7/24/2013

Praise for

Balance
The Business – Life Connection

"Jim Cusumano's book *Balance: The Business – Life Connection* is a wonderful reminder that through gratitude and the source of creativity, we have answers to life's greatest challenges and can truly find meaning, fulfillment, success, and our purpose in life."

—Deepak Chopra, MD
Best-selling author of *Spiritual Solutions*
Chopra Center for Wellbeing
Carlsbad, California

"Here is a genuinely useful book that's also a delight to read. It's business and life seen through the eyes of one of the most remarkable people you will ever meet, a true Renaissance Man. Jim Cusumano has already packed several amazing lives into the one he's living—scientist, entrepreneur, rock singer, family man, philanthropist—and he's just getting warmed up! *Balance: The Business – Life Connection* would be worth your time and attention if it were only a book of business wisdom, but it's a great deal more than that. I came away inspired by the degree of passion, compassion, and pure zest for living that one person can express in his journey through the world."

—Gay Hendricks, PhD
Best-selling author of *The Big Leap* and *The Corporate Mystic*
President, The Hendricks Institute
Ojai, California

"This is the story and the wisdom of a beautiful man—and a Renaissance Man at that. In *Balance: The Business – Life Connection* Jim Cusumano humbly shares what he has learned so that you can be inspired to your own greatness. Read it and reap!"

—Lance H. K. Secretan, PhD
Best-selling author of *The Spark, the Flame, and the Torch*
Former CEO of Manpower Inc.
The Secretan Center Inc.
Caledon, Ontario CANADA

"*Balance: The Business – Life Connection* is a delightful book. Unlike so many other books on finding happiness, this one does not preach. Instead, it takes you on a journey through a remarkable life. This journey will make you laugh, make you cry, but most importantly, make you think! *Balance* will help you approach the critical crossroads in your life in a whole new way, and help you find the "giants" in your life that can guide you through them."

—Professor Gary P. Pisano
Coauthor of *Producing Prosperity:*
Why America Needs a Manufacturing Renaissance
Harvard Business School
Cambridge, Massachusetts

"What a treasure this book is! Sharing his own mystical journey in *Balance: The Business – Life Connection*, Jim models for us the art of living your best life, and being aware of all the synchronistic moments that help lead the way! The golden threads of your inner calling … the things you feel you must do … are weaved together beautifully by the sharing of his extraordinary story!"

—Kathy Gardarian
Founder and CEO Qualis International, Inc.
Riverside, California

"Jim Cusumano's book is more than one man's incredibly successful multi-careered journey with delightful milestone markers in every chapter. It is a basic text brimming with wisdom for how to prosper in all of life's endeavors by developing hope, trust, compassion, diligence, perseverance, outside-the-box thinking, and wisdom. *Balance: The Business – Life Connection* is a 'must read' for every thoughtful person engaged in business at every level of enterprise."

—Rinaldo Brutoco
Founder, President and CEO World Business Academy
Santa Barbara, California

"From the oldest of ten children raised in a European ghetto in New Jersey, to rock star, scientist, corporate executive, entrepreneur, filmmaker, hotelier, philanthropist, mystic, and more—how does any one person navigate each of these endeavors with such gusto and success? In following his heart and soul, a true Renaissance man for all seasons, Jim Cusumano takes us on his exciting personal journey. In *Balance: The Business – Life Connection* he candidly and humbly shares what he has found to be a specific recipe for anyone to find their life purpose and passion, and thereby create success and happiness in both their professional and personal lives. I highly recommend this gem if you want to increase happiness and balance in your life."

—Dr. Rudolph E. Tanzi
Coauthor with Deepak Chopra of *Super Brain:*
Unleashing the Explosive Power of Your Mind to Maximize Health,
Happiness, and Spiritual Well-Being
Professor of Neurology Harvard Medical School
Director Genetics and Aging Research Unit,
Mass-General Institute for Neurodegenerative Disease,
Massachusetts General Hospital Boston, Massachusetts

"This is a book filled with energy, wisdom, passion, and tools that help with navigating the crossroads of life and making key decisions personally and professionally. In *Balance: The Business – Life Connection* Jim Cusumano tells the inspirational story of his life as he navigates a multifaceted journey as a rock star, scientist, corporate executive, entrepreneur, and hotelier. His path is truly a remarkable one, and the lessons he shares are universal."

—Richard Seewald
Partner, Alpha Associates
Zurich, Switzerland

"Jim Cusumano is one of those rare individuals who have been able to reinvent themselves several times, and excel at what they do every time. In *Balance: The Business – Life Connection*, he shares his 'secret sauce' and offers it in a way that everybody can apply to their own life plan. But this book is not about Jim, it is about the reader! His personal discoveries and wisdom are useful tools to help you live a life filled with happiness and high levels of accomplishment."

—James C. Blair, PhD
Founder/Partner, Domain Associates
Princeton, New Jersey

"*Balance: The Business – Life Connection* is an unusual title for an unusual book by an unusual man. Jim Cusumano is not the typical scientist, or typical rock star, or typical entrepreneur; my goodness, how would the word 'typical' even apply to these different and rather antithetical professions and skills? He writes in engaging and lively style, sharing with the reader his life's experiences, invaluable lessons from his journey of life. His experiences, such as interacting and learning from the ten 'giants' who influenced him so much, are captivating as well as full of gems. Jim's so many lives give you the impression there are different people within them, each one of them with unique life experiences; his reflections—not dry lessons, but on the contrary alive and full of energy—take you step by step into simple but profound principles of living the right way and enjoying a full life. When you have finished reading Jim's book, you will want to meet him in person. I was lucky to have met him and grateful to cross paths with such an unusual and fun, full-of-life, man."

—Professor Menas Kafatos
Author of *The Conscious Universe*
Dean Schmid College of Science & Technology
Chapman University, Orange, California

"Reading *Balance: The Business – Life Connection* reminds me that true Renaissance Men still exist. It is fantastic to experience all of Jim's lives, his love for his family and friends, his passion for learning and growth, and his drive for making the world a better place. The most amazing thing for me is that he so eloquently makes us believe that we can do these miracles as well. Even more so, he gives us a foolproof manual to do exactly so. Now I don't have an excuse not to try."

—Jan Sykora
Chairman of the Board, Wood & Company
Prague, Czech Republic

"Jim Cusumano is a person who has given a lot of time and thought to studying the major issue of our modern time: how, in this age of specialization, can a person give his or her life work broader meaning? He not only writes about it, but he lives it. He is a person who makes the community around him better. *Balance: The Business – Life Connection* is a worthy distillation of his philosophy and will benefit whoever reads it."

—Weston Stacey
Executive Director, American Chamber of Commerce
Czech Republic

"Jim is a student of science, philosophy and spirituality—a unique blend of mind, heart, and intuitive energy. Achieving success by any measure in life, love, and business adds weight to his assertions that a life worth living serves others as much as yourself. This makes his book an important one for our times. So many people spend hours of their life without experiencing the joy of finding true purpose and passion. They pursue material goals that provide only temporary happiness and perhaps some pain relief. Jim is a living example that it can be done! In reading *Balance: The Business – Life Connection*, you journey with him through life and share his lessons, and through that journey learn how to uncover your own path of purpose and passion. You will feel like you know Jim and you will in turn discover more of yourself. I thoroughly recommend this book to start your own adventure, no matter what your age!"

—Liam Forde
Founder, The Zone: Winning Cultures in Business, Monaco

"Jim Cusumano has ingeniously gifted us with not only the inspiration to a life of passion, purpose, and success, but he has laid out the strategic road map for us to follow. And we know that his system works, because he has walked the talk in his own life, many times over. Only a small percentage of humanity takes the leap necessary to love their calling. The result is a society that is searching for happiness outside of itself. *Balance: The Business – Life Connection* alone has the power to not only elevate one life, but our entire society as a whole."

—Allison Maslan
Author of *Blast Off! The Surefire Success Plan
to Launch Your Dreams into Reality*
CEO, Allison Maslan International, Cardiff, California

"I recently had the distinct pleasure of observing Jim with his six-year-old daughter, Julia, as she excitedly showed him a cricket she had found, gently cupping the little creature in her hand. He gave her all the attention, interest, and encouragement that reflect who Jim really is. With his gift for touching the spirit of others, it is not surprising that the adventures he has pursued in both his personal and professional lives have met with significant success. *Balance: The Business – Life Connection* is Jim living in words and actions. I highly recommend his book to everyone."

—Maryles Casto
Founder, Chairman & CEO Casto Travel
San Jose, California

"*Balance: The Business – Life Connection* is a book from a man who has gone through a lot. For readers who are embarking upon a similar path, this will be an interesting read. How to start again, how to gain, how to lose. How good things come as a by-product of a great calling."

—Tomáš Sedláček
Chief Macroeconomic Strategist, ČSO Bank
Prague, Czech Republic
Former Advisor to President Vaclav Havel
Author of *Economics of Good and Evil: The Quest for Economic Meaning from Gilgamesh to Wall Street*

"In a world in which so many people seek balance, meaning, and connectedness in life, Jim Cusumano provides a tangible and inspirational road map. Using his own remarkable life experience, *Balance: The Business – Life Connection* shows us how we can live our lives to the fullest. It is a very human story that made me laugh and made me cry, but most of all it motivated me to embrace more deliberately my own path of life discovery."

—Helene D. Gayle, MD, MPH
President and CEO, CARE USA
Atlanta, Georgia

Balance

Balance

The Business–Life Connection

James A. Cusumano, PhD

SelectBooks, Inc.
New York

This edition published by SelectBooks, Inc.
For information address SelectBooks, Inc., New York, New York.

First Edition

ISBN 978-1-59079-960-4

Inspirational Leadership® is a registered trademark of Lance Secretan

Library of Congress Cataloging-in-Publication Data

Cusumano, James A.
  Balance : your business--life connection / James A. Cusumano. -- 1st ed.
     p. cm.
  Includes bibliographical references.
  Summary: "Author draws from his success as a Rock 'n' Roll star, research scientist, corporate executive, Silicon Valley entrepreneur, and holistic hotelier to provide a template for creating a successful business along with fulfillment in our personal lives. He demonstrates ways to identify and unleash the passion and individual power to find our purpose, including service to others"--Provided by publisher.
  ISBN 978-1-59079-960-4 (pbk. book : alk. paper)
  1. Success in business. 2. Success. 3. Work-life balance. 4. Quality of life. I. Title.
  HF5386.C93 2013
  650.1--dc23
                                        2012044255

Interior book design and production by Janice Benight

Manufactured in the United States of America
10 9 8 7 6 5 4 3 2 1

For Inez

My wife, my lover, my best friend,
and the inspiration for this book

Books by James A. Cusumano

Freedom from Mid-East Oil
(with coauthors Jerry B. Brown and Rinaldo S. Brutoco)

Cosmic Consciousness: A Journey to Well-being, Happiness and Success

CONTENTS

FOREWORD

During your life, you will have many acquaintances,
but true friends you will count on one hand.[1]

—CHARLES A. CUSUMANO, SR.

BEFORE PUBLISHING MY BOOK *Letters to a Young Entrepreneur,* I asked Jim to review the manuscript and give me his input and critique. Of the many comments that I included in the final version of my manuscript, one stands out as defining Jim so well. It was in relation to my chapter "Companions in the Journey," where I emphasize the importance of deep trust in effective and successful business collaborations like the one he and I enjoyed over three decades of building companies together. He said: "To be honest, I sometimes fought with my ego throughout our decades together. However, in my moments of truth, I always knew that you were more important to me than the insecurities teasing my ego and certainly that our bigger vision for Catalytica was really what mattered." These words epitomize Jim and characterize the wisdom that he shares with us here.

In these pages you will gain an understanding of the pivotal personal characteristics that make for good leadership and the so important recognition that we are one and the same person in our private lives and in the conduct of our business affairs. His lessons are so consistent with what I most admire about Jim and his life story:

He embodies passion.

As Jim points out repeatedly in this book, *passion* is a key element of happiness and success. Certainly he has embodied this in everything that he has undertaken, and it seems to gives him boundless energy. I still remember how in spite of a skiing accident, cast and all, he proceeded to board a plane to join me in one of our early but key negotiations. The overarching mission we were on was all that mattered, regardless of discomfort or inconvenience.

He exudes enthusiasm.

Whatever he is undertaking, Jim does with excitement. It is hard to resist his "wake," and as a result it is easy for others to follow him and join in the journey. This is very much the mark of good leadership. Often, when several of us would see problems in tasks, his attitude that nothing is impossible usually won the day.

He listens.

In spite of his enthusiasm, Jim was never oblivious to the concerns of others. The reason he and I became such an effective duo was because there was such deep respect between us that even if we heard contrary ideas or approaches to our own, we internalized the other's perspective. So much of life is this give and take, this dance, enriching the outcome and the joy of the journey.

He inspires by doing, not by talking about it.

Jim is all life at all times. He plunges in fully. Even when we were addressing very specific business issues, they became a full part of him, not just a part to be tackled from 9 to 5. He dedicated his full attention to what he was engaged in and time was subsumed to the task at hand.

It is not surprising that the messages that permeate this special book embody these characteristics. They are presented in a very personal way, drawing on specifics from Jim's many endeavors, and creating an underlying message that a fulfilling life and a successful business go hand in hand and draw on the same fundamental personal traits and drivers. They rely on each of us finding our innate talents, and through that process discover our purpose in life and follow it faithfully. Honesty with ourselves is then reflected in our honesty with others, a key hallmark of good leadership—what Jim calls *Inspired and Conscious Leadership.*

Jim has done a great service by collecting these important reflections of a full life that has spanned many diverse careers and endeavors, and distilling them into *Balance.* The lessons he draws upon apply to all of us, regardless of our chosen profession or avocation. They contain fundamental concepts that can increase our happiness and our effectiveness, and simultaneously help make this a better world.

—RICARDO B. LEVY, PHD
Los Altos, California
ricardolevy.com

PREFACE

And when you want something all the universe conspires in helping you to achieve it.[2]

—PAULO COELHO

I HAVE HAD THE GOOD FORTUNE, or karma, to find a number of special opportunities along my life's journey. These opportunities always occurred at critical crossroads or turning points. I could have gone "left" or "right." I made choices, but the final outcome was not obvious at these decision points and often did not unfold until many years later. How do you make these challenging decisions with limited information?

I propose that there is always an "omen," usually an incisive occurrence that suggests the direction you should take, or perhaps a wise person who knows which path is best for you to create meaning and fulfillment in your life. Meaning and fulfillment encompass not only your business career, but also extend to your personal life as well. In fact, it is a continuous bridge of balance between these two important sectors of your life that is the source of long-term fulfillment and happiness.

As you will see in reading further, I am in the midst of my "Fifth Professional Life," having progressed from a 1960s' rock star with the Royal Teens in my youth to a scientist and a corporate research executive with Exxon; then to cofounder and chairman of a Silicon-Valley-based public company, Catalytica, Inc.; next to becoming the founder, CEO, and executive producer of Chateau Wally Films, a feature film company; and currently—but hopefully not finally—with my wife and business partner, Inez, to becoming the renovator and owner of Chateau Mcely, an internationally recognized castle hotel and spa, located just outside Prague in the Czech Republic.

I made some mistakes along the way, but learned a few things as well: most ostensibly how to see or uncover the "omens" at critical decision points and how to pursue these interests with the balance necessary to find meaning, fulfillment, and success in both my personal and business lives.

As a consequence, I have often been encouraged to share my thoughts about the fruits of my journey with the idea that others might find value in my experience and perspective. I offer you here my learnings and my discoveries.

My overarching goal in writing this book is to provide a means to help you find or enhance your fundamental purpose and passion, and in doing so to create a more meaningful and fulfilling life. While I have dealt extensively with my thoughts and experience in creating both a successful persona and professional life, I have particularly emphasized the latter. However, I have found that to create long-lasting fulfillment and happiness, it is absolutely necessary to pay diligent attention to both parts of your life in order to create the necessary balance.

If you take your valuable time to read this book, you deserve to know something about my personal and professional experience and the credibility of my recommendations. I wrote "Part I: My Story" because I would like you to have a sense of my source, my inner core, my "essence" as events unfolded throughout my personal and professional lives and led to my thinking and conclusions.

The central message I want to share with you is this: in the big picture, life is short, no matter how long you live. Yet I firmly believe that all of us were meant to live our lives to their fullest and most of us want to do so. You are likely among a large fraction of humanity that has evolved to a state of consciousness which enables you to make important contributions to the physical and consciousness evolution of our universe. That's why you are here, and there is no greater personal satisfaction on this planet than to being in the thick of doing so. If you are not yet on a path that takes you in that direction, please don't lose the opportunity. The reward will be beyond your greatest expectations.

I believe you came into this world with a specific set of skills that allows you to make unique contributions, both socially and professionally. I call this your personal "Essence;" ancient alchemists called it your "Quintessence," the Fifth Element beyond Earth, Fire, Water, and Air, also referred to as the *Aether* that links everything in the universe. These skills differentiate you from other people in your social and professional circles. You intimately sensed these capabilities when you were somewhere between the ages of five and fifteen. You didn't think in these terms but, believe me, you felt more than a tug in a direction that told you something fundamental about the direction of your life course and how you could contribute to the universe and its continued evolution. When people follow this path, they find their life purpose, generating high levels of physical and emotional energy to fuel their innate passion to create a better world. By balancing these powerful new-found forces within our persona and professional lives, the natural by-product during this journey is ALWAYS long-lasting abundance and personal fulfillment. Could there possibly be a better course of action?

But too often through unfortunate circumstances, such as ineffective and misleading advice concerning our life's journey from someone who may have meant well, or perhaps from some other source of modern day social hypnosis, we are steered in a direction that does not draw heavily on our fundamental Essence. As a consequence, we find we are not yet on the path of our Life Purpose. Have no fear. Even if your unique capabilities have been submerged over the years by other preoccupations, you can recapture them. This has been accomplished by many people. And it doesn't matter at what stage in your life you are in; it's never too late to find your way and be where you were meant to be.

The late multibillionaire Ray Kroc, the son of modest Czech immigrants, grew up in Chicago and tried all kinds of jobs, including jazz band pianist, waiter, and traveling salesman, among many others. Ray was fifty-two years old when he finally discovered his life purpose and founded the global McDonald's franchise. Harland "Colonel" Sanders was sixty-five when he launched the global Kentucky Fried Chicken franchise. Don't waste your time trying to live another person's dream—no matter whose dream it is—it can't be done. That course almost always leads to disappointment and an also-ran life.

If you don't remember what your fundamental Essence is, I will show you how to rediscover it. If you are patient, you will see the process does not take long. All it requires is commitment and a modest level of tenacity. Once you are clear as to what your Essence is, you can use that skill set to find the proper place or profession for you in this world—something that calls to your very soul—whether it is to be a loving mother and/or housewife, a carpenter, or an inspirational CEO of a large enterprise, or perhaps founder and leader of your own adventure. This is the true path to long-term happiness, abundance, and fulfillment. I pray that I can provide you with the means to find and follow that path. At a minimum, my hope is that for each chapter you read, you get at least one solid idea of value, something you can hang on to that will make a positive difference in your life.

I am truly confident that when you know intimately and unquestionably your purpose in life, you will connect that purpose to a need in this deeply challenged world to make it a better place in which to live. This will generate an intense personal passion. And that passion will ignite immense physical and emotional energy to enable you to deal with uncertainty which is the source of incredible creativity. When all is certain or completely known, there is no room for creativity. And the converse is true; the greater the uncertainty, the greater the level of potential for creativity. Your creativity will blossom into successful innovation, whether it is expressed directly in your own life or in the lives of others.

Perhaps this path will take you to a large company, or result in your founding a venture of your own. You will discover that the creativity-innovation process is always rewarding and provides a deep sense of gratitude; and *gratitude always leads to long-term fulfillment and happiness.* The greater your sense of gratitude, the greater your level of happiness. That's the way our universe works.

One final note: I have worked diligently to be pragmatic and specific in my discussions throughout this book. However, at another level you may recognize a more ephemeral message. We live in deeply challenging times. As a result, there are increasing numbers of people around the world who believe that there is a more fundamental and timely need for purpose, passion, and innovation involving all levels of the human spirit. These visionaries—scientists, philosophers, spiritualists and others—maintain that humanity is on the cusp of a quantum shift to a new paradigm. This new way of being honors our interconnectedness and recognizes the unsurpassed power, potential, and creativity that this connection brings to individuals and to the "whole." This book provides a roadmap for those who embrace this change and seek to facilitate this transition and the promise of a better future for all.

I wish you great success. If but one person reads this book and as a result is helped to find long-term happiness, I will share in that happiness. That's just the way it is; we're all connected. If you find this book of value, please tell your friends or, better yet, loan them the book. And if you care to do so, I would also be most appreciative if you were to share with me your thoughts as well.

—JAMES A. CUSUMANO
Chateau Mcely
289 36 Mcely Czech Republic
Jim@ChateauMcely.com
www.ChateauMcely.com
www.BalanceTheBusinessLifeConnection.com
December 21, 2012

ACKNOWLEDGMENTS

A LIFE OF BALANCE, PASSION, AND FULFILLMENT is *never* lived alone, and it's never due to the genius of a single person. Many people believe that Albert Einstein worked in total solitude while developing his General Theory of Relativity. Not so. If you were to see a list of all of the brilliant scientists he consulted with his thought experiments and mathematics during his efforts on relativity, you would be amazed at the extent of the list and the contributions by others. And so it has been throughout my much humbler life. Therefore, I would like to recognize the geniuses and giants in my life who helped me find balance, passion, and fulfillment, and as a consequence to be able to share with you what I have learned.

I am deeply and sincerely grateful to Ricardo Levy, my dearest friend and business partner for more than three decades, and one of the most important "giants" in my life. Ricardo, author of the very incisive, *Letters to a Young Entrepreneur*, meticulously performed the first edit of my manuscript and put it in much more interesting and readable form. As my "second memory" he checked me on dates, facts, and figures concerning the myriad of experiences we lived through together as entrepreneurs. I also thank Nancy Sugihara, my editor at SelectBooks, who tirelessly and constructively helped me to develop the final manuscript into a cogent product. Her patience with my questions, comments, and strange grammatical constructs is most commendable. However, if there are any errors of substance they are all mine.

Sincere appreciation goes to my good friend, Rinaldo Brutoco, founder, president and CEO of the World Business Academy in Santa Barbara, California. Rinaldo showed great interest and support for what I had to say, and introduced me to Bill Gladstone, my talented, experienced, and most effective literary agent, and a successful author in his own right. Bill also helped me in challenging, understanding, extending, and distilling my ideas by introducing me to some of the talented authors and thinkers he represents, including the genius of Ervin Laszlo and Ruben Papian.

As expressed in chapter 1, my exciting journey would never have happened were it not for a number of "giants" in my life. In particular, there were ten who either created or identified critical forks or turning points in my life path, and helped me choose the right way to proceed. Not an easy task! I pay special homage to the first two of these "giants," my mother, Carmela, and my father, Charles, who were respectively responsible for inspiring my "lives" in entertainment and science.

I want to recognize my nine brothers and sisters—Maria Teresa, Charles Anthony, Salvatore Joseph, Camille Jeanne, Grace Cecilia, Lisa Ann, Thomas Edward, Tina Marie, and Donna Gina. As a family, we were always one and there for each other; that's the way of La Famiglia Siciliana. However, growing up together and to this very day, we have often disagreed and sometimes even vehemently argued our personal beliefs concerning matters pertinent to a life of fulfillment and happiness. Just be a "fly on the wall" for an hour or so at one of our holiday dinners and get-togethers—Mamma Mia, what a debate! However, this creative tension has been a source of introspective learning for me and for that, I am deeply grateful to each of them.

In the entertainment field, it was Bob Baran and the late Buff Decker two excellent New Jersey born-and-bred guitarists who launched me into an incredible multi-decade magical foray in rock and roll music. And what a blast that was!

I was introduced to the magic, intricacies, and challenges of moviemaking by my incredibly creative and talented deceased wife, Jane Cusumano. As writer and director, Jane was the prime driving force behind our feature film, *What Matters Most*. For production and distribution of the film, Sherry Lansing, then CEO of Paramount Pictures, provided guidance and counsel that helped me immensely in my role as Executive Producer. As busy as she was, she found time to point me in the right direction to develop an effective strategy to commercialize the film. Two talented women, two "giants" in my journey.

My serious commercial adventures in science and technology began with a PhD in physical chemistry under the inspirational guidance of the late Professor M. J. D. Low at Rutgers University, and were subsequently guided by the mastery of "Three Wise Magi"—Ricardo Levy, the late Michel Boudart, and the late John H. Sinfelt. In addition to Ricardo, Michel was also my business partner and an internationally recognized professor of chemistry and chemical engineering at Stanford University. John was a Senior Scientist at Exxon, where during my tenure with that company, he counseled me on how to be most effective at industrial research and successfully commercialize the fruits of my efforts. This knowledge paid off handsomely in guiding the growth of Catalytica, the company Ricardo, Michel, and I founded. Hopefully, within the pages of this book I have done justice to John's critical role.

I would be remiss without mentioning my appreciation and admiration for the work of Dr. Lance Secretan. Over many years of experimentation and development, Ricardo and I uncovered what might be called today "Conscious

Leadership." *We thought of it as "Inspired Leadership" because to inspire others, we found that you must first be inspired yourself.* It was a powerful lever for our professional and personal successes. Years later, I discovered Lance's work on Inspirational Leadership®. I have used his articulation of Inspirational Leadership® in parts of this book because it neatly packages what Ricardo and I discovered as Inspired Leadership, and it adds a valuable complement.

I am indebted to the many reviewers who read my manuscript and provided valuable insight, as well as their endorsement.

I want to recognize my three talented daughters, Doreen Nelsen, Polly Cole, and Julia Cusumano for their challenging questions and comments over the years. Their creative ideas sometimes seem to come "out of left field," but because of that, they are always a source of learning and enlightenment for me and have contributed to the substance of my thoughts on leadership and fulfillment.

Finally, and *most* especially, I express my deep love and sincere gratitude to my wife, Inez, *the* "giant" in my life; she has consistently provided her support and actually suggested the means to get this book written. Inez has demonstrated time and again that genius, creativity, internal and external beauty, humility, and a deep concern for the "whole" are beautiful and powerful virtues, and it truly is possible for them all to reside simultaneously and comfortably within the soul of a single individual.

There were so many others along the way, too many to mention here, who gave generously of their time, support, recognition, and nurturing. More than ever, I'm deeply convinced that no one does anything of true significance in this world, alone. Sir Isaac Newton got it right—success is achieved easier from the "shoulders of giants."

Yes, Virginia, we are all connected!

The Road Not Taken

Two roads diverged in a yellow wood,
And sorry I could not travel both
And be one traveler, long I stood
And looked down one as far as I could
To where it bent in the undergrowth;

Then took the other, as just as fair,
And having perhaps the better claim
Because it was grassy and wanted wear,
Though as for that the passing there
Had worn them really about the same,

And both that morning equally lay
In leaves no step had trodden black.
Oh, I marked the first for another day!
Yet knowing how way leads on to way
I doubted if I should ever come back.

I shall be telling this with a sigh
Somewhere ages and ages hence:
Two roads diverged in a wood, and I,
I took the one less traveled by,
And that has made all the difference.

Robert Frost
Mountain Interval, 1916

PART I

My Story

CHAPTER 1

ON THE SHOULDERS OF GIANTS

If I have seen further, it is by standing on the shoulders of giants.[3]

—SIR ISAAC NEWTON

KEY CONCEPTS

- Everyone encounters a number of critical crossroads in their life— distinct possible paths—each with a formidably different outcome.
- Prior to each of these decision points, you will meet a guide: a learned, emotionally-skilled "giant" who is there to help you decide the right path to take. They are *always* there, but not *always* easy to recognize. You must listen carefully!
- By carefully listening to understand—not just to hear—the message from these "giants," you can make the right choice and play out your destiny with balance fueled by passion, and resulting in long-term fulfillment and success.
- It is difficult to identify and benefit from these "giants" if you are com- pletely driven by your ego and forgo the power of your Personal Con- sciousness.
- If you connect with "giants" along your life journey, you will eventually recognize the true gift of your existence and purpose in this universe.

I NEVER THOUGHT OF MY LIFE as anything extraordinary until my sixti- eth birthday when, over an expensive and memorable bottle of 1982 Chateau Petrus, I took a long and deep retrospective look at my personal and professional lives. Yes, there were some incredible challenges along the way, like giving up near term financial freedom from a career in rock and roll music for what turned out to be an exciting career in science, but began with a job that paid only $15,000 per year; or more poignantly, losing my wife in the prime of her life to breast cancer. Yet, as I swirled and slowly sipped that glass of rich Bordeaux, and looked past those few black clouds at the true radiance in my life, I felt an overwhelming sense of gratitude. I mentally relived the string of magnificent opportunities the universe had presented to me, and for just a brief moment I thought, "Wow, what luck!"

But it wasn't just luck. This I can assure you. As Louis Pasteur noted over a century ago, "Luck favors the prepared mind." And my mind was indeed prepared at key junctions. But, like Isaac Newton, I for sure "stood on the shoulders of giants," people whose intellectual and emotional intelligence helped me make important decisions at key turning points in my life. They were truly "angels" who were there at the right moment to guide my personal and professional success, and they could see my prospective future clearly, more clearly than I could.

There were a number of these "giants" in my life, but there were ten special ones who made important observations and contributions at key crossroads in my journey. Sometimes they even created these important decision points. And of course, as baseball great Yogi Berra was fond of saying, "When you come to a fork in the road, take it!" It made the difficult decision at these junctures easier and clearer than if these guides had not been there for me. It also provided perspective on how to keep my life in balance, namely by not violating those fundamental values that became part of my internal compass, my access to my conscious "true north." All of us meet these people throughout our life's journey as we reach these crossroads. *The path we take—left or right—determines just how meaningful and fulfilling our life will be. The key is to recognize these "giants," to listen carefully to* **understand,** *not just to hear their counsel, and then in a moment of quiet introspective truth to recognize how it all fits together.*

I won't elaborate on all of my critical crossroads. Providing a few will hopefully make the point of how important these junctures can be in your life. These examples also illustrate how my life unfolded quite naturally into five distinct professional adventures.

Sicilian-American Life in New Jersey

As the oldest of ten children—six girls and four boys—one child born approximately every two years, I was constantly, unwittingly, and annoyingly faced with responsibility. "Madonna mia! You're the oldest; you've got to set a good example! Capisce?" my father would say. If I heard it one more time, I thought I would scream!

Until I reached the age of twenty, it seemed like Mom—Carmela Madeleine Cusumano—was perpetually pregnant. Now ninety-one years of age, and a beautiful woman by any standard, she was and still is a soft but positive and effective force. That's the way it is in most Sicilian families. She is a devout Roman Catholic who attends church more frequently than every Sunday and prays the Rosary daily, not only as a means of personal prayer and meditation, but also to request from the Blessed Mother a list of spiritual favors petitioned to Mom by family, friends, and neighbors. Generally the requests come from people who are at least Catholic in name, but occasionally some dribble in from non-Catholics, and once, even from an atheist! "What the hell, just in case, and after all, it can't hurt," he said! It's reminiscent of Nobel laureate physicist Niels Bohr's response when quizzed about a "good luck" horseshoe hanging over the entry to his summer home, "I'm not superstitious, but, you know, they say it works even if you don't believe!"

It usually happens something like this: "Carmela—oh please—my boy Joey, he's not doing well in school, and he has an important final exam coming up," or "My daughter Maria is having her first baby and she's not feeling well," or "My husband, Mario, is having surgery" or some other special need. She never says no, and somehow she almost always works a miracle. She is without question the "Mother Teresa" of our family, and a premier practitioner of Quantum Cosmic Consciousness,[4] which maintains that all things in the universe are interconnected, and if you learn to access the subtle spiritual power that exists in all of us, you can "touch" anything and anyone and work what appears to others to be a miracle.[5]

My father, Charles Anthony Cusumano, who died in 2004 at the age of eighty-four, was the first "giant" in my life, even though we never really got along well. He was a hard working, World War II disabled veteran, physically and emotionally damaged by hell and havoc from his experiences fighting Japanese soldiers in the jungles of New Guinea. I tried desperately to understand him. "How do you trounce around the jungles of New Guinea, watching your buddies get shot or blown to bits, and doing the same to Japanese soldiers, and ever return to a normal life?" I would say to myself. Unfortunately, I was too young. It didn't help much.

He had a lot of good qualities. He was intelligent, charismatic, generous, loyal, and entertaining. And he loved his wife and children. But for three decades, our family ignored, enabled, and lived with his alcohol addiction until, finally, as a consequence of a severe family upheaval at my brother Tom's wedding and Dad's subsequent self-admission to an addiction center, he beat the ethanol demon for the next two decades until his death. Today, we would call it post-traumatic stress disorder. But those kinds of illnesses were unknown, or at least not recognized, immediately subsequent to World War II. That was much before the era of our great "Prozac Nation."

"Charlie," as he was known to friends and family, was enigmatic and a person of paradoxes. Everyone loved him. Yet a simple event, such as someone inadvertently pushing him in line or cutting him off on the road, could send him into a tirade. All ten of us had varying degrees of a love-resentment relationship with Dad. During his alcoholic years, if you were late coming home he could easily whack you on the back of head, send you to bed without dinner, and then later, when he thought you were asleep, kneel beside your bed asking God and you for forgiveness. Everyone who knew Dad before the war said that he wasn't the same "Charlie" who set sail for the South Pacific. Like many GIs he suffered from the scars of war, which in his case seem to have been manifested in depression and unresolved anger.

Mom was three months pregnant when Dad left for New Guinea. I was a "honeymoon baby," conceived out of Sicilian passion, born nine months and two weeks after they were married. Both my maternal and fraternal grand-parents prayed daily that I would not be born early—"Who knows what the neighbors would think!" I met my father for the first time when I was nearly three years old. It was not a great start. A few days after his arrival home from New Guinea, he was feeding me Gerber's baby custard from a jar as I sat playfully in my highchair at the kitchen table. I decided after a few spoonfuls that I didn't want any more of the gelatinous stuff. "Jimmy, open up," he commanded in true military style. He had been discharged as a staff sergeant and had all of the attendant mentality of that office. I stared back and forth between his intense eyes and the bottle of custard, keeping my mouth closed as tight as a vice. At the time, I had no idea what he might do. "Jimmy, open up," he continued with increased intensity. No way, I didn't want any more. Then, in a flash, he jammed the spoon into the bottle and catapulted the remaining custard into my face. To this day, I'm not crazy about custard.

After Dad's re-enlistment and post-war military stints in Hollywood, Florida, and Phoenix, Arizona, he transitioned out of the U.S. Army Air Corps—the predecessor of the U.S. Air Force—and we moved back home to 714 Van Buren Avenue in the northern corner of Elizabeth, New Jersey, immediately adjacent to what would eventually become the runways of today's Newark International Airport. There, we crammed into a small three-bedroom flat downstairs from my maternal grandparents, Giovanna and Salvatore Catalano, who owned the two-family home.

Mom and Dad had one bedroom; the girls occupied the second one, and the boys the third. I have vivid memories of my brothers Chuck, Sal, and me sleeping in an old queen-size bed. A king size would not fit in the room. When going to sleep, invisible lines of demarcation were drawn between each of us in the bed, and God help you if you crossed the line!

We never lived in a home with more than four small bedrooms, even when there were nearly ten of us running around the house in addition to several friends of each of us, who for some reason liked hanging out at the overcrowded Cusumanos' home. Perhaps it was because my father was entertaining to them, or maybe because my mom was always a good listener to problems—but probably because we had the best Italian food in all of Elizabeth, bar none! Eventually, Mom wrote a cookbook, self-published it, and to this day it is a prized possession to those lucky ones who have a copy.

My grandparents were hard-working, first-generation immigrants from Cammarata, a modest village in Sicily not far from the infamous, wealth-adorned city of Corleone. They owned the home we lived in for the first fourteen years of my life, so the rent was reasonable. However, there was a strong friction between my grandmother and my father. She constantly reminded him that we were too many kids, who made too much noise, and used too much water, electricity, and heating fuel. My dad dreamed of the day he could afford his own home and put some distance between him and my grandmother.

For job security, he took a life-long position in civil service at the U. S. Post Office. But it was to be a deep thorn in his side for his entire professional life. For many decades the Elizabeth post office was run and controlled by the Irish, who were not particularly appreciative of Italians, and especially Sicilians. The Irish "earned their stripes" after immigration to the greater New York area. Italians came next, so they were on a lower rung in the pecking order within the multinational neighborhood in which we lived and worked. Dad had incredibly high native intelligence. He would consistently achieve the highest grade in postal examinations, only to be deeply frustrated and angered when he was unfairly passed over time and again by an O'Brian or a Riley who had a lower grade. His IQ and EQ were both high, but that didn't matter under the prevailing circumstances. He was still one of those "damned dagos," a "wiry wop," or a "greasy guinea," and a host of other deprecating slang labels we faced in the neighborhood where we lived. As a youngster, I ended up in more fist fights than I care to remember because of this prejudice.

But Dad was very well liked in the Italian community and he was often approached by, shall I say, "Sicilian acquaintances," who wanted to help him get his just due. He always graciously refused; that just wasn't his way. The only exception was when he allowed Giuseppe Carlotta, whom we kids called "Uncle Joe," use our flat and telephone a few nights a week to run his numbers business. That was when things were really tough and we needed the extra income. But Uncle Joe eventually left our place because we had a two-party telephone line, and the other party threatened to turn Mom and Dad in to the police.

After "addition" number four (Salvatore Joseph), Dad began to work part-time jobs at night and on the weekends to make ends meet as night manager at a local supermarket and also tending bar—where he met his alcohol nemesis. With so many children and one modestly-paying job in the family, we were poor by today's standards. We just didn't know it, since a number of the folks in the neighborhood were in a similar situation. One occasion out of many paints this picture vividly.

It was the winter of 1952 on an early February morning during a vicious New Jersey snowstorm. Dad did not have the 14 cents—that's right, 14 cents—necessary to take the Number 30 bus from North Elizabeth where we lived to the Elizabeth Port Post Office where he worked at the time. It was a good five miles by bus. He was too proud to walk upstairs and borrow the money from my grandmother. She would have given it to him, but not before she reminded him that he gave her daughter too many children. So he walked to work that morning and then home in the evening during one of New Jersey's worst blizzards on record.

I vividly recall watching the 1997 Academy Awards on TV, when Roberto Benigni, the star, screenplay writer, and director of *Life is Beautiful,* won the award for Best Foreign Language Film. Benigni jumped up on the backs of the seats, and to the storming applause of an ecstatic audience made his way to the stage. After a number of sincere and heartfelt comments he turned to the audience, many of them with tears of joy and admiration in their eyes and said, "And I especially want to thank my parents for the gift of poverty!" There is something to Benigni's comment. Not only does poverty provide a driving force for success, but, by necessity, it motivates you to be flexible, resourceful, and creative in developing solutions to tough problems.

However, let's be clear, there must be a "way out," and it helps immensely to be loved and have emotional support, and to live in a country with broad professional potential. In this respect, a young teenage rebel in terrorist-stricken Somalia does not have nearly the amount of possibilities as a youngster from a poor Sicilian family in a North Elizabeth ghetto.

This was my wellspring; this was my source; this was my early training ground. It set the stage for what would eventually be the unfolding of five professional lives—so far—in the fields of technology and entertainment.

* * *

Life No. 1—Rock and Roll Star

Mom was the "giant" who set me on a path to my first professional career, an entertainer in the rock and roll music business. At age ten, growing up in a large family of very modest means, I needed a job to support my personal habits—baseball picture cards, a fast bicycle, "cool" clothes, and gasoline-powered model airplanes. Also, it was an unwritten rule in our family that by the time we were ten-years-old, each of us had to work part-time. Half of our take went to help the family, and the other half we could keep for ourselves. Dreading the cold New Jersey winters, I wanted an "inside job," so that I could set myself free from my newspaper route and selling fruits and vegetables in the Elizabeth Italian market on weekends.

Listening to Mom play "The Isle of Capri" on an old rickety upright piano she had owned since childhood gave me the idea, which she encouraged, particularly after hearing me play the same tune completely "by ear." I wanted to start a band to play for school dances. That would be so cool! Since Mom was an amateur musician as a youngster, it wasn't difficult to convince her that I needed piano lessons, even though it was a significant financial challenge for our family. But Dad, being the creative charmer that he was, convinced Vince O'Brian, one of his army buddies—yes, he was Irish and a professional band leader—to teach me "the real thing."

I attended one thirty-minute private lesson each week, learning to read and play contemporary music, using a "fake book"—a wonderful invention for working musicians. A fake book contains music for several hundred popular songs. For each song, it displays the right-hand melody line as single notes, and for the left hand, simply states the appropriate chord just above the melody line. The fake book was a godsend for this student-in-a-hurry-with-a-mission, but everything else I learned from Vince, including swing bass and how to fill in the correct complementary notes for a given chord while playing in octaves with the left and right hands. It was pure magic; I became a working "musician" in less than three years and joined Local 151 Musicians' Union!

At that point, my close friend and schoolmate Buffy Decker and his cousin Bob Baran, both excellent guitar players, asked me to join their rock band "Little Orbie & The Satellites" as their keyboard player and lead singer, playing proms, weddings, Bar Mitzvahs, smoke-filled saloons, you name it. I loved '50s' rock and roll music—especially the four-part harmony songs by many of the successful black groups like the Flamingos, the Moonglows, and the Cleftones. It was my dream to meet them and sing on the same stage.

I soon began writing my own songs, mostly ballads. Living just across from Manhattan, it was easy to take the bus and venture into the City once or twice a month to sell my songs to "Doo Wop" groups, mostly in Harlem, Brooklyn, and the Bronx. It didn't occur to me to copyright my creations, so I simply sold them outright. The return was anywhere from a "buck" to $15 a song—a lot of money in those days for a teenager.

It helped that I occasionally played musical accompaniment for some local well-known singers such as Rosie Greer from nearby Roselle. Rosie was the famous three-hundred-plus-pound tackle who played for the New York Giants at the time and sang "Moonlight in Vermont" like a meadowlark. The first time he came to our home in Rahway, New Jersey—we finally bought our own home—he could barely fit down the stairs to our basement where I kept my piano. Mom still talks about "That huge giant who nearly broke the stairs to our basement!" Rosie eventually became a preacher and is best known for his counsel to O. J. Simpson during that infamous trial.

I loved the energy of Manhattan and spent quite a bit of time there searching for music opportunities. The late 1950s and early 1960s was a "dry" period for me, and I found it difficult to come up with good saleable tunes, probably because I was also focused on doing well in school. But finally I hit upon a tune I really liked a lot. It was called "My One True Love," and I recorded it as a demo with a fabulous girls group called "The Three Pennies"—two sisters, Pat and Muriel Fox, and their close friend Joanne Esposito. They sang such close three-part harmony that it almost sounded like a single voice.

One Saturday afternoon in early 1961, excited about selling my latest "surely soon-to-be-hit," I enthusiastically entered the famous 1650 Broadway Building in Manhattan. That and the nearby Brill Building became the

East Coast pinnacle for the birth of great rock and roll music. The songs that came out of those two buildings were an integral part of what became known as the "Brill Sound." Carole King, Burt Bacharach, Jerry Leiber and Mike Stoller, Phil Spector, Neil Diamond, and many others were all there. In one building, you could write, publish, demo, record, and sell a song. It was a true "one-stop shop."

After a number of "not interested" rejections, I walked into the office of Leo Rodgers, a well-known record producer, who had a number of successful early rock groups signed under his wing. One in particular, whom I admired immensely, was The Harptones, featuring the incredible lead voice of Willie Winfield. Willie and his group recorded "Sunday Kind of Love," "My Memories of You," and the unforgettable, incomparable "Life Is But a Dream." What great songs, what a magical group! Leo liked "My One True Love," and asked if I would consider him as my manager. I agreed, and then and there signed my first recording contract, although I had no idea what I was signing at the time. I tried to convince Leo to have the Harptones' record "My One True Love," but somehow, to my great disappointment, it never got off the ground, either with them or any of his other groups.

However, some good did come out of my relationship with Leo. With "Dino" as my stage name, I eventually became the lead singer for the Royal Teens of "Short Shorts" fame, who had been managed by Leo. The original group came to him as the Royals, but he renamed them the Royal Teens and established their identity leading up to their recording of "Short Shorts" in 1958. The group had difficulty creating an equally successful second hit, and after many changes in personnel, eventually disbanded. I introduced Leo to the band I was singing with in New Jersey, and after a few changes, we had a solid group re-established as the Royal Teens. We recorded several songs, which either never were released or were short-lived after their release. It was very disheartening. We continued to play nightclubs and colleges on the East Coast and traveled during school holidays and summers. Finally things were about to change—at least, I thought so.

Our group had not had any real visibility since 1962, the year we released "Short Shorts Twist," a neat sound that played off "Short Shorts" and Chubby Checker's hit, "The Twist." When first released, it was on its way to becoming a smash hit in New York City. The infamous disc jockey Alan Freed from WABC and WINS radio in Manhattan, who coined the words "rock and roll" in 1951 while working as a DJ in Cleveland, was a close friend of Leo Rodgers and also of Leo Gray, our booking agent at the William Morris

Agency. Freed played "Short Shorts Twist" like crazy. He loved the tune. Immediately after its release it became the "Hit Record of the Week" on WINS. Everyone was convinced "Short Shorts Twist" would go "Gold" But our "high" was short-lived since Freed was directed by WINS management to discontinue playing rock and roll music altogether and transition to Frank Sinatra's recordings and a similar genre. That was a real letdown, as we only needed a couple more weeks of play on WINS to establish the sales momentum we needed for a national hit.

But in time there was a silver lining. Executives at Musicor Records remembered "Short Shorts Twist," which they liked very much, so they offered us a deal in December of 1969. We signed a recording contract with Musicor to arrange and record an album called *Newies but Oldies* produced by the talented Les Paul, Jr., son of the famous Les Paul, jazz guitaris and inventor of the solid-body electric guitar. The album was a clever idea dreamed up by our co-producers, Bill and Steve Jerome—a compilation of sensational hits of the 1960s done in the style of the 1950s. The concept had never been done before so the producers were nearly neurotic about us not discussing the album with anyone until its release.

In early 1970 "Newies But Oldies" was released with a single from the album, as well. The "A-side" was "Hey Jude" by the Beatles sung to the melody of "In the Still of the Night" by the Five Satins. The "B-Side' was "Smile A Little Smile for Me, Rosemarie," done like "Little Darling" by the Diamonds. It was a real spoof and great fun to record, and was played heavily by DJs at WABC in Manhattan.

With the "Teens" I traveled and played with many of the great pioneers of rock and roll—Chuck Berry, Fats Domino, Little Richard, Bo Diddley, Jerry Lee Lewis, and just about every Doo Wop group from Dion and the Belmonts to the Flamingos and Harvey and the Moonglows. Although, as with many of the early rock groups of the '50s and '60s, we did not receive the financial compensation we should have, it sure beat delivering newspapers and selling fruits and vegetables in the Elizabeth Italian market. And it enabled me to help out at home and buy some of the things I had dreamed about, like a cherry-red 1957 Chevy convertible with all the trimmings. Life was great!

Alan Freed was a key factor in keeping the Royal Teens on the charts. We played for minimal wages at his shows and at "The Camelot," a popular Manhattan nightclub owned by Roulette Records rock mogul Morris "Mo" Levy. Freed was often the "front man" at the Camelot, so much so that for the longest time I thought he owned the club. He eventually was the prime target and victim during prosecutions for the 1950s' "payola scandal" involving cash payments or gifts from record companies to disc jockeys, and he was subsequently banished from New York radio. He moved to California and sadly soon after that died at the age of forty-three, a penniless alcoholic.

Fortunately from an early age I had always had a passion for science and technology. As a consequence of this, I studied chemistry and physics, while continuing to play with the Royal Teens. I graduated in 1968 from Rutgers University with a PhD in physical chemistry. While I was an undergraduate at Rutgers, most of my professors allowed me to travel and miss classes as long as I took all of my examinations and kept my grades at a respectable level. Bob Baran, who with my schoolmate Buff Decker, recruited me at age fourteen to play with "Little Orbie and The Satellites," and who eventually played lead guitar and then bass for the Royal Teens, was also a Rutgers student. We were both chemistry majors and became lifelong friends.

During performance intermissions Bob and I would study physics and calculus in the back room of the nightclubs at which we were playing, while the rest of the group ran after girls, always wondering about our priorities in life! We learned to get along on three to four hours of sleep per night, most of it taken in the car ride home; we took turns driving. There was no other choice if we wanted to continue to play with the group and go to school at the same time. I have no idea as to how we managed our lives physically and emotionally. A few points are clear—we were passionate about what we were doing; we ran nearly constantly on adrenalin; and we were young.

There were a couple of times in graduate school when I nearly gave up on science, not because I lost interest, but because the temptation tugging on me was almost irresistible. One instance in particular occurred in 1965 shortly before completing my doctorate. I received a call from Frankie Fanne who was in Las Vegas. Frankie was a booking agent whom I knew quite well and who was close with Frankie Valli and the Four Seasons, at that time one of the most successful recording groups in America. Bob Gaudio, who wrote most of their music and who was the group's keyboard player, was one of the original Royal Teens and participated in writing "Short Shorts." Frankie said the Four Seasons had lost Nick Massi, their bass player and background singer, and Nick had been immediately but temporarily replaced by a good friend of the Four Seasons, the successful singer, writer, and producer Charlie Callelo. Charlie could not stay with the group, so Frankie wanted me to audition for the position, which he claimed was essentially a "shoe-in" after speaking with Bob Gaudio.

I spent two difficult days in deep thought before calling Frankie back and telling him that I was incredibly grateful for the opportunity, but I would not pursue it. His long silence on the telephone betrayed his disbelief. The Four Seasons eventually recruited Joey Long (LaBracio), an excellent singer and talented classically-trained musician, who was also from Elizabeth. Much of this episode is portrayed in the current highly successful Broadway play, *Jersey Boys*, which tells the life story of Frankie Valli and the Four Seasons.

I instead chose to go to work for Exxon immediately after graduation as a research scientist, receiving less than 10 percent of the annual starting salary I might have received with the Four Seasons, excluding recording royalties. I never looked back and never regretted the decision. The instant elevation to stardom and the money were most attractive, but it just wasn't my calling. It wasn't my passion, and it would have put my life completely out of balance.

Life No. 2—Exxon Scientist in Corporate America

My father was the first of the "giants" in my technological professional life. He created a critical crossroads for me, and through his support, helped me make what I know in retrospect was not only the right decision, but one of the most important in my life.

It was Christmas 1950 and the streets of Elizabeth were packed with snow. There were no snowplows in our neighborhood. I am sure that the tax rate there was too low to justify the costs, compared with Elmora and Westminster, the swank sections of Elizabeth that received all of the city services they needed. Besides, we didn't have a car at the time, so it really didn't matter to us. We went everywhere by bus, or someone else drove, and more often than not, we just walked. It was nothing for our family to walk five miles to visit someone. So, as usual, we walked the three miles to Blessed Sacrament Church for Midnight Mass that Christmas Eve. When we returned home, we were allowed to open one gift before going to bed and our subsequent Christmas morning celebration. I chose the big box wrapped in Kraft® brown paper, carefully constructed from old grocery bags. Mom could really make a present look tempting with just the right touch of colored ribbon.

When I removed the wrapping, there it was—a Gilbert chemistry set carefully packed in a blue metal box that opened just like a book. Now mind you, I was only eight years old and could barely read the instruction booklet. What parent today would buy their eight-year-old son a chemistry set, especially one such as those sold in the 1950s before formation of the Environmental Protection Agency and its safety laws? A typical set had all of the ingredients necessary to make interesting products such as gunpowder (flowers of sulfur plus charcoal powder plus potassium nitrate), rocket propellants (zinc powder plus flowers of sulfur), a spontaneous igniting fire bomb (glycerin plus potassium permanganate), or perhaps nitrogen triiodice (iodine crystals plus ammonium hydroxide), which when carefully dried would violently explode at the tickle of a feather.[6] My father wanted me to be a medical doctor, so he thought the chemistry set might inspire me. And inspire me it did—but not to a career in medicine. However, this inspiration wasn't completely obvious to me until I really immersed myself into the exciting process of creating something new.

After a month or so in my basement laboratory, concocting pyrotechnics and stink bombs, I checked out from the public library a neat recipe book of "1001 Useful Formulas" that described products I could make from common chemicals available at the hardware and drug stores. I decided to "go into business." My mom and dad were supportive, and my grandparents tolerated me; they let me build my laboratory in their basement, hoping I would someday become a scientist who would solve many of the world's problems—especially theirs, e.g., arthritis, "agita" (Sicilian dialect for indigestion and gas pains), and especially intense malaise and sleepiness after three glasses of their homemade wine.

My father asked a friend of his to make me some "company" labels—O & O Research Labs ("O" stood for "organic")—and I started making and packaging my own soap, cosmetics, inks, cleaning fluid—you name it—and then selling my "products" in the neighborhood. Most people, either feeling sorry for me or just intrigued by a young "scientist," began to buy more and more of my products. It was fantastic! I loved the idea that I could make things in my lab, and that somebody was actually willing to pay for them! The money was important, but the positive feedback for something of value that I had created was even more important and incredibly invigorating.

I even learned about technical service. I convinced Mrs. Semeresky, who owned the neighborhood grocery store, to sell my ink and I would split the profits with her. Actually it was revenues—I had no idea if I ever made a profit. I supplied her with bottles that were twice the volume of Waterman's Ink and sold them for half the price. I was going to put Waterman's out of business! The kids who went to the neighborhood schools bought all the ink I could make. In those days we used fountain pens, the kind that had an internal rubber bladder that was filled with ink from a bottle by depressing and then releasing a small external lever on the barrel of the pen.

And then the problem arose. I still remember the formulation. I mixed 1 gram of ferric ammonium chloride with 1 gram of sodium ferrocyanide in fifty milliliters of water. This makes a beautiful deep Prussian blue color of ferric ferrocyanide. Then heat the solution to about 75° C and add 0.5 grams of gum Arabic, and 1 drop of calcium hypochlorite solution (bleach) to prevent the gum Arabic from growing bacteria. Cool and then bottle and you have an ink that is as good as any other that could be bought at the time. At that early stage in my technology career, I couldn't even read the chemical names, so I called the ingredients "ferric ammunition chloride" and "sodium ferro-nod-egg." On this occasion I was making a big batch of ink, and I must have inadvertently added too much gum Arabic. Its function was to help the ink adhere properly to paper.

Mrs. Semeresky subsequently received numerous complaints that pens were clogging and then not working at all. She said if I didn't fix the problem, there would be no more sales of my products in her store—ever! I collected all of the clogged pens, brought them home, and in Mom's kitchen boiled them in a large pot of water for an hour. That solved the problem. I returned the pens with two free bottles of properly prepared ink. It was a big success, and the kids in the neighborhood continued to buy my ink. Mrs. Semeresky was proud of me, and I guess I was, too.

I didn't quite realize it at the time, but *I had discovered that I loved using technology to create a product that brought real value to the world, and that someone wanted badly enough to be willing to pay for it.* I then and there decided that I wanted to be a scientist, not a medical doctor, as my father might have wished. However, to be fair, over the years he was supportive of my chosen endeavor. This was a critical crossroads in my life, where I could have gone right or left. I didn't ask for the chemistry set. It was handed to me by the universe through my dad's good intentions. I could have taken the other path, and used the chemistry set for a time and discarded it, just as I did with many of my other toys. But, somehow, I chose to listen to where this adventure wanted to take me.

In retrospect, I believe quite strongly that it was my father's emotional support that led me in that direction. He was proud of my little neighborhood entrepreneurial business. He also constantly encouraged me to study science and mathematics. Over the years, I spent nearly every penny I earned to build and maintain a large laboratory in our basement. I had a number of severe near misses, explosions—you name it—that I survived. However, in one instance, just barely. It was chemistry that led me at age ten to nearly leave this world.

It was a cold winter Tuesday afternoon on January 22, 1952, a date etched in my memory for reasons you will appreciate in a moment. I stayed home from school with a cold. Dad gave strict orders to Mom that I was not to play in my lab in the cellar. He said it was too damp and I would only get sicker. But as the day wore on, I was bored and asked my mom if I could bring parts of my chemistry lab up to the kitchen table and do some experiments while she ironed clothes in the same room. She reluctantly agreed. In the course of the afternoon, I did several experiments as Mom put up with the yucky odors that permeated her kitchen as she was preparing garlic-laced tomato sauce for that evening's pasta. However, not even garlic could compete with the aromas I created as a byproduct of my alchemy!

At one point I was formulating a new potent spot remover that I wanted to sell in the neighborhood. I had trouble opening a tube filled with finely-divided calcium hypochlorite powder, a potent bleaching agent. The corked tube had been tightly sealed by the manufacturer with a cellulose plastic coating. I pulled on the plastic-coated cork with all of my might. Then, as best I can remember, it popped and the calcium hypochlorite, which apparently had been vacuum-packed, exploded into my face as air rushed into the tube and displaced the vacuum. It temporarily blinded me and filled my nose and throat with a fine white cloud of the poisonous substance. Fortunately, my mom was there and she immediately flushed my eyes and had me drink some water. I could barely stand up. Mom was crying and simultaneously praying rapidly and incessantly in Sicilian dialect to the Blessed Mother.

We didn't own a car, so she immediately called for an ambulance. Unfortunately, none was available because at 3:45 p.m. that same afternoon American Airlines Flight 6780, intent on landing at Newark Airport, crashed into a home adjacent to the Elizabeth River, just missing Battin High School for girls by but a few feet. Every available ambulance in Elizabeth was sent to the crash scene. Mom was able to get my Aunt Mary who lived nearby to take me to the emergency room, where, in view of the plane crash, I was lucky to get medical attention. I was examined by a physician and an eye doctor, both of whom said I appeared to be fine, having regurgitated most of the poison in route to the hospital.

However, the next day, whether caused by the toxin or not, no one would ever say, my appendix burst in my stomach leading to a severe case of deadly peritonitis. I was hospitalized and given very little chance to survive and as a good Catholic boy received Last Rites. Months later, I was told by my grandparents that this experience was among the most difficult times for my parents.

I was delirious with fever for nearly seven days, but during the early morning hours on that last day, my high fever broke and I awoke in the morning reasonably alert and saw Mom sleeping in a chair at the foot of my bed. I had finally responded to the huge levels of intravenous antibiotics that were flowing through my veins and was on my way to what would be a very slow recovery.

It was also chemistry that apparently led me to have what is known as a "near-death experience" during my illness. I told my mom that I had a vivid "dream" in which I was walking in a brightly-lit tunnel and had met several people who said they were waiting for me, but that it was too early for me to be there. One of them appeared to be my grandfather who had died a couple of years before I was born. When I explained this "dream" to Mom and the doctors, the doctors smiled, but Mom's reaction was very different. With tears of joy streaming down her face and her Rosary in hand, she confided that she didn't think it was fantasy and that I was very lucky to have recovered. Much to the surprise and concern of friends and family, I continued my deep passion for chemistry and with the full support of my parents.

Eventually it was the right choice at this crossroads that enabled me to generate the passion to pursue and receive my doctorate in physical chemistry, to become a Director of R&D for Exxon, and to found two public technology companies. To this day I continue to publish articles in magazines in an effort to educate the public on the challenges of key issues such as energy security and climate change. All of this sprang forth from personal passion created by that first Gilbert chemistry set and by the unwavering encouragement of my dad and others. The next chapter in my life was about to be written.

While in graduate school I continued to play with the Royal Teens, and in 1966 we decided to work the summer at clubs in Manhattan—the famous Wagon Wheel and the Peppermint Lounges on West 45th Street—and at the Jersey Shore—Augie Hoffman's Hoffman House in Point Pleasant, the Pillow Talk Lounge in Asbury Park, The Pinup Lounge in Atlantic Highlands, and at the Beachcomber and Chatterbox in Seaside Heights. Through a set of circuitous circumstances—there are no coincidences in this universe—I received an opportunity to work during that summer as a Research Fellow at Exxon with an internationally-recognized scientist, Dr. John H. Sinfelt. John had been nominated several times for the Nobel Prize in Chemistry for his groundbreaking work in catalytic science, the subject of my doctoral thesis. I couldn't pass up the opportunity, so I decided for that summer I would work at Exxon during the day and sing with the Royal Teens at night, sleeping mostly on the weekends! It was a most amazing and exhausting summer.

I was very careful to keep my scientific and entertainment lives quite separate. It was the 1960s and I didn't want anyone to think I was a "flake." Would anyone in science take me seriously if they knew I was working in rock and roll, and in fact, you might even posit the converse, as well? But, as author and *New York Times* columnist Thomas Friedman likes to say, "The world is flat!" And I saw that quite clearly one afternoon, a couple of weeks after starting my summer fellowship at Exxon.

John assigned me to share an office with Dr. David J. C. Yates, a some-times-thorny, Cambridge-educated Englishman and one of the bright international stars in catalytic and surface science. That afternoon Dave was desperately trying to convince me that thermodynamics, when applied to catalytic surfaces, was nonsense. Of course I was two years into my doctorate thesis doing just that kind of "nonsense." As I defended my case in higher-pitched tones, John walked in and began to facilitate the debate so that we both saw each other's point of view.

A short time later, a pretty blond mail girl entered the office, and before she could place the mail on our respective desks, she exclaimed with excitement. "Dino, I saw you on TV last night with the Royal Teens. Can I have your autograph?" My jaw dropped, and before I could say anything, David and John inquired with authentic excitement in unison, "Who are you?" As it so happened they were both amused and impressed when I finally confessed the details of my story.

John taught me more about practical chemistry and physics in one summer than I had learned in my prior two years of graduate school. For that reason, upon graduating from Rutgers with my doctorate I decided to go to work at Exxon. I knew I would finally leave the Royal Teens, when my first daughter Doreen was born January 3, 1967. I felt I should get a full time respectable "day job." Besides, with an emerging family, I didn't want to go on the road again. That never works well in the long run, especially when you have young children.

So I accepted my first full-time day job on November 1, 1967, with Exxon as a research scientist in the Catalysis Research Group, the area I had worked in for my doctoral thesis at Rutgers—for the annual salary of $15,000. But it wasn't the money I was after; it was a chance to learn practical technology with the crème de la crème of research scientists and engineers in industrial catalytic science. I wanted to solve real-world problems and make it a better place to live. Since my involvement as a kid in my basement chemistry lab, I had come to love the innovation process—use good science to solve practical problems, and then through creative technology development, bring highly-desirable, valuable products to the market place. And Exxon was a great place to do just that.

At Exxon I learned a lot about commercial technology development, and within a few years, thanks to John Sinfelt, I became the youngest research director in Exxon's Corporate Research Laboratory. It was wonderful schooling, jam-packed with the best and brightest from only the top schools such as Harvard, Stanford, Columbia, MIT, and Cal Tech. At the time, I was the only graduate from Rutgers University in the Corporate Research Laboratory. The group I managed—Catalytic Science & Technology—was talented, productive, and responsible for creating hundreds of millions of dollars in annual revenues for the company, much of it based on John Sinfelt's science and inventions. It was a wonderful and truly enlightening experience. Several of our young team members went on to become famous scientists and engineers in the field of catalysis.

But the large corporate bureaucracy was too much for my entrepreneurial spirit—too many meetings, too much internal reporting, and too many "dog and pony shows." So in 1974, much to the disbelief of Exxon's President of Research & Engineering, who had told me that I was pegged for a vice presidency at Exxon, I gave up my enviable position as Director of Catalytic R&D, and headed west to California's Silicon Valley to start my own company. I made this dramatic move with two close friends, Ricardo Levy, an incredibly personable, bright, and successful research engineer from Exxon's Materials Science Group, and the late Michel Boucart, a world-famous catalytic scientist and Professor of Chemistry and Chemical Engineering at Stanford University.

I made this decision after numerous consultations with John Sinfelt, who was not only supportive, but encouraged me to follow "my dream"—even though he would personally feel the loss of my presence at Exxon. He was a very tall "giant" in my life journey. His selfless encouragement and counsel at this critical juncture in my life were one of the most significant factors for my subsequent success as an entrepreneur.

There were a couple of incestuous connections involved in this founders' triac. Ricardo received his doctorate in chemical engineering with Michel at Stanford, and Michel was one of Exxon's long-time, top consultants, especially to my group in catalysis. Exxon was not happy with the three of us when we chose to leave, and made it very clear on several occasions. I knew that we must be on to something important when the vice president of R&D threatened to compete with us.

Our new endeavor was actually precipitated one day early in 1974 when I had returned from a technical presentation to Neil Hakala, then the President of Exxon Research & Engineering. Our group had developed a new catalytic hydrogenation process that could make highly profitable products with projected annual revenues of $75 million. Neil listened carefully and graciously to my presentation and commented on the high quality of the work, and then within what seemed like a nanosecond said, "No interest. Exxon cannot afford the time and resources to play with products that yield only $75 million per year in revenues." In retrospect, he clearly was right.

Back in the laboratory, I lamented to Jim Costello, one of our research technicians by saying, "You know, I would love to take this technology from Exxon and start my own company. After all, $75 million per year is not a bad start!" Ricardo was in the lab using our computer system. All ears, he jumped up, pulled me by the arm into my office across the hall, sat me in my chair, perched on my desk, stared into my eyes with semi-contained excitement and said, "Did you really mean that you would like to start your own company?" A simple "yes" was all it took. It so happened that Ricardo, a brilliant chemical engineer from a successful, entrepreneurial, German Jewish refugee family in Quito, Ecuador, had been in preliminary discussions with Michel Boudart to start a company. My dear friend Ricardo Levy—one of the tallest, if not *the* tallest— of all the "giants" in my life.

On November 1, 1974, during the worst recessions since World War II, we walked out of Exxon with a simple strategic plan in our heads—start with consulting: the first customer would be the U.S. Government; then steadily transition to private industry and, hopefully, some day make our own products.

Ricardo and I had a dream. We had discovered our fundamental purpose deep down inside our very souls—we were experts in catalytic science and technology. We understood the rugged journey of taking a catalyst discovery in the laboratory through pilot-plant scale-up all the way to commercialization. We now understood that was our fundamental professional essence. And *we connected that capability with an urgent need in the world, one that could make it a better place in which to live—cleaner, lower cost products through catalysis, thereby helping to create a sustainable future.* We were passionate, we were on our way, we had absolutely no doubt we would succeed. The hell with the recession!

Life No. 3—Silicon Valley Entrepreneur

The year 1974 was a difficult one economically, worldwide. The country was smack-dab in the middle of the first Arab Oil Embargo. OPEC had announced that they would no longer ship oil to countries that had supported Israel in the Yom Kippur War. The United States, Western Europe, and Japan were especially affected. Interest rates in the United States topped 20 percent. The price of oil went through the roof and Americans lined up for hours at filling stations to buy a couple of gallons of gasoline. It was a real mess. But, somehow Ricardo and I were immune to these negative forces. Sure, we felt the pressure in our sales efforts, but we were convinced that during economically troubled times such as these there would eventually be a need for more efficient, cleaner, low-cost technologies to make fuels, chemicals, and pharmaceuticals, and our know-how in catalytic technologies would be highly valued. We just had to figure out a way to operate until that "eventually" arrived. The answer was consulting.

Having no external funding, Michel, Ricardo, and I each contributed a hard-earned $10,000, and started our company as a consulting group—Catalytica Associates, Inc.—with Michel opening doors for us, and Ricardo and I doing the work as full-time employees. Michel's help immediately won us two contracts worth a total of nearly $200,000, one with the U.S. Energy Research Development Administration (ERDA),[7] and the other with the Electric Power Research Institute (EPRI) in Palo Alto, California, where we located our first office at Palo Alto Square, close to Michel at Stanford University. We were only three employees, Ricardo, me, and a secretary.

We thought, "Wow, that kind of money should go a long way to taking care of our modest monthly salaries for quite some time!"

We were quite naïve financially in the beginning, but fortunately we were quick learners and became intimately familiar with cash flow management. ERDA and EPRI, like many organizations, do not pay until the work is properly completed, and even then not for a few months. Ricardo was forced to borrow money from his kind mother-in-law to pay our bills and salaries. But we quickly got the hang of things and after creating a line of credit with Silicon Valley Bank, we were on our way.

As an international star in the field of Catalysis, Michel made it easier for us to meet important government and corporate personnel and to attract and hire the world's most knowledgeable consulting associates, and ultimately super employees. He also was an incredibly bright intellectual filter and made it difficult for us to make any serious technical faux pas in the work we did. However, there were many years of distance between Michel on one hand, and Ricardo and me on the other. This difference in age meant that Michel wanted to see financial compensation sooner rather than later. After all, he was much closer to retirement age than Ricardo and I were. We never ever even thought about the concept of retirement and still don't. As young entrepreneurs in our early 30s, we also did not worry about compensation. Yes, after the first few years we paid ourselves fairly, but much more important to us was the fact that Catalytica was our "baby," and *we desperately wanted it to make the world a better place in which to live* That was the primal force behind everything we did. This difference in values was sometimes a source of tension between Michel and us, but through mutual respect we managed to get past the problems.

Michel was also a super-bright academic intellectual, and while both Ricardo and I thrived on science, we were commercially driven. The work we did had to address a market or, even better, create one. For example, we decided that strategically, as a means to generate greater revenues and profits, it would be beneficial to produce technical market-driven multi-client studies that were relevant to the concerns of industry at the time. As a consequence of the Arab Oil Embargo the world was in the midst of the last major energy crisis, so the first topic that Ricardo and I chose for a multi-client study was directed at increasing America's energy security. It was a technical analysis and commercial perspective for the conversion of coal to chemicals and fuels using the most up-to-date catalytic technologies. There was an abundance of government and corporate funding available for

R&D on this subject as the Western world tried to move out of the clutches of the oil-rich Middle East and toward energy independence.

Michel, on the other hand, lobbied strongly for us to do a study on what is known as chiral catalysis, the use of catalytic chemistry to produce only the truly active form of a drug molecule. Many drug molecules often exist as both a "left" and "right" hand form—the word "chiral" comes from the Greek word meaning "hand." These forms are referred to as the L-isomer and the R-isomer, respectively. Usually, one isomer is therapeutic, while the other may be either inactive or often has serious negative side effects. The thalidomide debacle of the late 1950s is a prime example of what can go wrong. The final drug, taken by pregnant women for morning sickness, was a 50/50 mixture of both the L-isomer and R-isomer of thalidomide. One isomer was indeed therapeutic, but the other turned out to be a teratogen, which caused terrible birth defects.

While chiral catalysis was and still is important, Ricardo and I felt that coal-to-fuels-and-chemicals as a means to minimize the United States' dependence on Middle East oil was more relevant and urgent at the time. We were right. It was too early for a multi-client study on chiral catalysis. Our first study on coal-to-fuels-and-chemicals became a global "best seller"—more than $2 million in revenues, and hugely profitable, especially for a company with low fixed costs and only a few employees. Furthermore, it gave us great credibility and brought about a number of additional contracts. Equally important, in carrying out these multi-client studies we were getting paid to analyze in detail important new technologies, thereby continuing our education concerning cutting edge science and global industrial problems and interests.

It was quite difficult at times, but with some luck and lots of hard work, our reputation began to take off and we were able to hire more members to our team. We became a world-recognized consulting group in the field of catalysis, and we saved our clients millions of dollars annually by improving their chemical processes. At the time, catalysis was responsible for nearly 25 percent of our global GDP, so we had an extensive market. As planned, we initially worked for the U.S. Government and quasi-governmental groups such as EPRI, but eventually we moved our efforts into the industrial sector. Clients included Merck, Pfizer, Atlantic Richfield Company, American Cyanamid, Johnson & Johnson Pharmaceuticals, Dow Chemical, Calgon, and many other Fortune 500 chemical and energy companies.

After a while it occurred to us that we were selling our experience, knowledge, and know-how too cheaply. We would improve a process for a company, saving them millions of dollars annually and get paid simply for our time. We decided to change our strategy. Up until that point, our growth was financed completely from profits. In 1983 we began raising venture capital to develop and commercialize our own technologies.

This was a difficult transition emotionally because it was the first move towards giving up the complete control that Ricardo, Michel, and I had as Catalytica Associates, now renamed Catalytica, Inc. However, it was the only way we could achieve our dream of creating valuable products that were manufactured, providing revenues even as we slept at night. The productive capacity of the company did not stop when our employees went home. *Most importantly, it also gave us an opportunity to make an even bigger positive impact on the world, and that really put fire under our already existing passion.* A product strategy also allowed us to achieve a greater return on our investment of time, money, and emotional energy.

Ricardo and I had excellent guidance from our board during that period, particularly from Paul Cook, founder and CEO of the multibillion-dollar Raychem Corporation; Carl Djerassi, a pioneer at Syntex Corporation and "father" of the birth control pill synthesis, as well as the founder and CEO of Zoecon Corporation; Ernest Mario, CEO of Alza Corporation and a former CEO of Glaxo Wellcome Pharmaceuticals; and Barry Bloom, Executive Vice President of R&D at Pfizer. These board members helped us chart our journey.

But perhaps one of the most influential of all was a true gentleman by the name of Tommy Davis, founder of the Mayfield Fund, and an early investor in Silicon Graphics, Amgen, Genentech, Immunex, and Tandem Computers. The Mayfield Fund was our first venture partner, providing us with $3 million in 1983. Tommy truly loved Ricardo and me; it was people who mattered to him. He would often say, "I'll take an "A" Team with a "B" idea any day over the converse!" Not that Catalytica had "B" ideas, but Tommy convinced his partners at Mayfield that since they did so well with their investment in Genentech, a world leader in *genetic engineering*, they might just do the same with Catalytica, a world leader in *molecular engineering* of catalysts. As it happened, he turned out to be right.

Between 1983 and 1993 we raised nearly $250 million in venture financing and divided the company into three business units, Catalytica Pharmaceuticals, Inc. (CPI), Catalytica Energy Systems, Inc. (CESI), and Catalytica Technologies, Inc. (CTI). All three businesses were directed at socially-beneficial, cost-effective products and processes—low cost pharmaceuticals made using environmentally-friendly processes; low cost sustainable energy systems; and in CTI we continued a modest segment of our initial strategy to use our extensive know-how in catalysis to improve existing processes, making them cleaner and lower cost.

We were creating "green" and sustainable technologies well before the terms were coined. *Our commitment and capability to develop commercial processes to manufacture products in a way that was lower cost and cleaner was what excited and motivated not only Ricardo, Michel, and me, but also our employees, especially when times were challenging. We knew we were making a positive difference in the world and that eventually that difference would bring an excellent return to all of the stakeholders in our company; not just to our shareholders, but also to our employees, our customers, our suppliers, our community—and yes, to the world.*

At CESI our Catalytic Combustion Team invented and developed the world's first practical, operating catalytic combustor system for gas turbines, expressly for the purpose of generating clean electricity. We had partner relationships with General Electric and Kawasaki Turbines and ran our system in a power plant in Santa Clara, California, for more than 1,000 hours with no problems. Because of the unique function of our catalytic system, we could produce electricity with essentially no formation of harmful smog-producing nitrogen oxides (NO_x), unburned hydrocarbons (UHC), and carbon monoxide (CO). The first time GE tested our XONON™ Cool Combustion system at their research facility in Schenectady, New York,[8] they thought that their NO_x measuring device was broken when it showed zero NO_x. They replaced the device with a new one only to find that zero NO_x was correct!

We managed an initial public offering on the NASDAQ stock exchange in February 1993. With several follow-up public and private offerings over the next five years, we raised well over $200 million to make Catalytica one of the most successful and fastest growing companies in Silicon Valley. By far, our efforts in pharmaceuticals (CPI) exceeded everyone's expectations. CPI grew, in less than five years, from several people and no sales to 1,800 people, nearly $500 million in revenues, $60 million in free cash flow, and a market value of close to $1 billion.

This clearly was not your usual organic growth. We ramped up reasonably rapidly through the acquisition of three state-of-the-art manufacturing plants, our prize site being the Glaxo Wellcome plant in Greenville, North

Carolina. Although we went out of our way to hire the best people, I was still amazed how quickly we became proficient across the entire spectrum of research, development, engineering, manufacturing, clinical support services, sales, and marketing. Much of this success had to do with our Inspired Leadership management style (a form of Inspirational Leadership® as discussed in chapter 7) and continual team building throughout the company. From our roots as a research organization we became a fully-integrated pharmaceutical manufacturing company.

At one point we were producing more than fifty major drugs for the top pharmaceutical companies throughout the world. For example, we made nearly the world's supply of GlaxoSmithKlein's AZT, or Zidovudine® the primary effective treatment for AIDS at the time. We also produced Zyban®, a smoking cessation drug, Wellbutrin® for treating depression and anxiety, and Lanoxin®, a digoxin drug for cardiovascular disease. We manufactured a large number of over-the-counter drugs including the world's supply of Neosporin®, Sudafed®, and Actifed®—billions of tablets per year. We became the "gold standard" for pharmaceutical manufacturing and the envy of all of our global competitors.

Acquisition of the Glaxo plant was a "miracle" in itself. In 1996 Catalytica had annual revenues of about $20 million. We wanted to expand our effort in pharmaceutical manufacturing, and at that point our strategy called for development of processes for the manufacture of just the active ingredient in drugs; the so-called "bulk active." However, when Glaxo acquired Wellcome Pharmaceuticals, and it became clear that for political reasons they were going to sell the Wellcome plant in Greenville, North Carolina, rather than Glaxo plants in the United Kingdom, we were ready.

Greenville was one of the most advanced pharmaceutical plants in the world, totally self-contained, manufacturing everything from the bulk active ingredients in drugs to the final dosage form—tablets, liquids, injectables, and so forth. They even produced their own packaging. At the Greenville facility Wellcome had just built one of the most advanced design sterile plants in the world for the production of injectable drugs. We wanted to buy the Greenville plant, but it meant a huge change in strategy—a move from producing only the bulk active ingredients in drugs to manufacturing the final packaged drug. If successful, we would become one of the world's largest pharmaceutical contract manufacturers in the industry.

Our board, Ricardo, and I struggled with this, but in a moment of truth and after discussion with key "giants" on our board, we decided to go for it. It is quite a story in itself, as to how little ole Catalytica competed with several international multibillion-dollar companies for the plant. But in the end, we won the bid, and with the help of Howard Hoffen, the Managing Director of Morgan Stanley Capital Partners, we raised the $300 million necessary to purchase the plant and Howard became an important and productive member of our board.

The more than 1,500 employees at the Greenville plant were ecstatic that Catalytica won the acquisition because we saved their jobs, whereas our bidding competitors would likely have dismissed a large number of them and brought in their own people for operations. Ricardo and I were also overjoyed. I vividly recall the closing celebration in Greenville, which was televised, attended by numerous political dignitaries and all of the employees. There were more than 2,000 people in the large auditorium where senior executives from Glaxo Wellcome, Ricardo, and I gave our presentations. Just before my turn at the podium, I leaned over to Ricardo and told him not to be too surprised at what I was about to do. He looked at me quizzically, but without concern; we had immense mutual trust. After my presentation, I sang a cappella "The Impossible Dream" from the musical *The Man from La Mancha*. When I finished, a number of the employees were in tears, and I received a standing ovation. It had been a challenging win for all of us, and we were all grateful for the outcome. It was among the most powerful moments in my professional career.

Within four years this acquisition raised Catalytica's annual revenues of about $20 million to almost $500 million. The employees in Greenville loved us and we loved them. However, merging two very diverse cultures, a reserved one from the deep South with that of our go-get 'em team in Silicon Valley was not easy, but we succeeded. Ricardo and I practically lived in Greenville for the first year, and we made a number of transfers in both the easterly and westerly directions.

I personally dedicated nearly full time to our efforts in pharmaceuticals by taking on the role of Chairman and CEO of Catalytica Pharmaceuticals, Inc. in addition to my role as Chairman of the parent company, Catalytica, Inc. To help things transition more smoothly, we hired Dr. Gabriel Cipau as President and Chief Operating Officer of CPI and eventually promoted him to CEO of CPI. Gabe had managed the Greenville facility several years before when it was owned exclusively by Wellcome Pharmaceuticals. We also did lots of team building and within a year we were doing well, especially as we continued to negotiate significant additional contracts with Glaxo Wellcome and other major pharmaceutical companies to manufacture some of their important commercial drugs.

The next step in our strategy was to use our technology to assist major pharmaceutical companies in their development of low-cost, clean processes for manufacturing new drugs that were in clinical trials. You see, when an organic chemist decides to synthesize a potential new drug molecule, he or she is not concerned at that point with the manufacturing process before the drug proves to be successful. If, in the end, the drug molecule proves to be potent and clinically acceptable, often the laboratory synthesis might require ten or more complicated steps, using toxic raw materials. Even if each step were to provide 90 percent yield of the desired product, 0.9 multiplied by itself ten times means a final yield of only 35 percent. Sixty-five percent of the raw materials are lost.

However, using our catalytic know-how and technologies, we were often successful in developing a manufacturing process that might have three or four steps, and also eliminated the necessity for highly-toxic or dangerous starting materials. This inevitably had significant economic and ecological benefits.

We were successful with a number of new drugs. For example, our technology helped in the development of the manufacturing process for Aricept®, the Eisai-Pfizer drug for treating Alzheimer's disease. Pfizer was so impressed that they invested $15 million into CPI as a means of accessing our technologies and know-how for the manufacture of their new drugs.

Catalytica Pharmaceuticals became so successful that in 2000 one of our largest competitors, the multibillion-dollar DSM Pharmaceuticals in the Netherlands, made our shareholders "an offer they couldn't refuse." In 1997 DSM had competed against us unsuccessfully for the purchase of the Greenville plant. This time they succeeded: we sold Catalytica Pharmaceuticals, spun off Catalytica Technologies, and kept only the remaining Catalytica Energy Systems as the Catalytica mainstay on the NASDAQ. We made our shareholders very happy.

Tommy Davis's intuition had been right on target. We provided a significant financial return to the Mayfield Fund and to all of our investors. In time, we merged CESI with RENEGY, a renewable energy company. Thanks to the "giants" who provided sound guidance and counsel to Ricardo and me, Catalytica's technologies and tentacles touched hundreds of companies, millions of people, and made this a better world. It was a special gift for me to be part of the adventure.

Life No. 4—Movie Producer

At roughly the same time that all of these changes were occurring, I "retired"—
I really dislike the word—from Catalytica to help my screenplay-writer wife,
Jane, set up Chateau Wally Films and produce a movie entitled *What Matters
Most*.[9] The film was to be directed by Jane[10] and it co-starred Polly Cole,[11]
then Polly Cusumano, my youngest daughter at the time, and an actress living
in Los Angeles. Ricardo stayed on at Catalytica to negotiate the sale of the
pharmaceutical business and to manage the remaining business unit, CESI.

My early retirement was driven primarily by personal reasons. Jane
had just fought a nasty battle with breast cancer, having faced intensive
chemotherapy, a mastectomy, breast reconstruction, and numerous rounds
of alternative medicine in Mexico and other parts of the world, since these
therapies were illegal in the United States. Her cancer was finally in remis-
sion. I was determined to help her get healthy again and to pursue her
dream. Jane wanted to direct her film. I knew that would be a tough sell with
major film distributors. We moved to Ojai, a small artists' community in
southern California near Santa Barbara, where we bought a heritage home
on a small horse ranch. Horses were Jane's hobby. She competed regularly
in dressage and was quite good at it.

Ojai was also a respite for many of the big-time Los Angeles movie
stars, producers, and directors. They all had second homes there, including
Reese Witherspoon, Diane Ladd, Laura Dern, Larry Hagman, Tim Burton,
Ted Danson, Jake Gyllenhaal, Jerry Bruckheimer, Malcolm MacDowell and
Anthony Hopkins. Some of them were our neighbors and good friends and
wonderful counselors for the neophytes that we were in this challenging
business called "movie making." We were particularly indebted to our good
friends and next-door neighbors, Robert Hunter, former CEO of PepsiCo
Food Systems, now an author and movie producer; and his wife, actress
Diane Ladd, and her daughter, actress Laura Dern. They were always available for advice and counsel and made sure that Jane and I were at many of
their parties to meet the rest of the Hollywood crowd from Ojai.

I introduced Jane and her screenplay, entitled *What Matters Most*, to
Sherry Lansing, then Chairwoman and CEO of Paramount Pictures. I had
met Sherry through David Koch, who sat on our board at Catalytica. David,
who dated Sherry when they were both single, and his brother Charles own
and run Koch Industries, the second largest privately-held company in the
U.S., an energy and chemical conglomerate with annual sales of more than
$100 billion.

Sherry loved the screenplay, and she liked Jane, but there was no way she could accept Jane as the director. It was the typical Hollywood "chicken-and-egg" syndrome—you can't become a director unless you're well known, and you can't become well known unless you direct successful movies. I discussed this with Jane and she and I thought, "Well, maybe we should bring it to the other studios?" But that would have taken months to get through the bureaucracies, especially as we had no contacts at the other studios. *And that was the critical crossroads, but I wouldn't know it for about a year—do we go to other studios, or do we bite the bullet and fund the movie ourselves?* Although the budget for the film was not small by any means, we had enough funds since Catalytica had gone public a few years earlier, so financing wasn't an issue. But the probability of getting any return on our investment, by Hollywood statistics, was less than 1 percent.

Jane and I wrestled with the problem for three days and nights and then finally, after a long discussion, she proclaimed with great insight and commitment, *"Let's start our own film company and shoot it ourselves. So what if neither of us know anything about making a movie or running a film company; it can't be that difficult."* In that moment of truth, I knew that she was right. She was the "giant" in my life at that moment in time. And that's exactly what we did.

She auditioned numerous actors, and finally in addition to our daughter Polly, she chose Chad Allen, Gretchen German, Tamara Clatterbuck, Marshall Teague, and Jim Metzler as the lead actors. All were "second tier" but amazingly capable actors and had been featured in a number of major films. I hired Charla Driver, a competent and highly-experienced producer. She in turn helped me hire Richard Munchkin, a director, a technology-based professional blackjack player,[12] and probably the only person with any directing experience who would have agreed to be Jane's advisor and consultant. Charla and "Munch," as we called him, hired all of the other personnel required to make the film. As executive producer I took charge of the financial controls.

On September 1, 2000, we were three days away from leaving for Amarillo, Texas, twenty miles from the three hundred-person town of Vega, located near historic U.S. Route 66 where we would shoot the entire film. Jane returned that afternoon from her oncologist visit in the Bay Area with the devastating news—her cancer had returned with a vengeance—stage IV—and she needed to go on chemotherapy immediately. How serious is that? There is no stage V. I asked her what she wanted to do. "I'm going to make that film, that's what I'm going to do!" I called her doctor to set up for chemotherapy treatments in Amarillo at the Harrington Cancer Center and she would direct the film as planned. To this day, I'm sure her doctor agreed and was supportive because she knew there was not much of a probability that Jane would beat the disease.

We went to Texas; we made the movie, and Jane received chemotherapy every Friday morning, right before shooting. It was a very difficult time for all, but the actors and crew were inspired by her tenacity and courage. Some days she could barely walk, and we were often shooting twelve to fifteen hour days.

Jane helped edit the film, and when finished, I immediately brought it to Sherry Lansing. She loved it, but it had no big name actors and therefore it was not for Paramount. On May 1, 2001, immediately after completion of the final cut of the film, Jane viewed it on the big screen at a studio that I rented in Los Angeles. She was amazingly proud of it, and rightfully so. A month later, on June 1, 2001, Jane lost her battle with breast cancer. She died in my arms at Cottage Hospital in Santa Barbara, California. Even though we saw it coming, it was devastating for Polly and me.

The news of Jane's death spread rapidly after a long article about her appeared in the Los Angeles Times. Sherry called me almost immediately from her car as she was on her way to LAX to fly to Venice where Paramount was shooting *The Italian Job*, starring Mark Wahlberg and Charlize Theron. After offering her sympathy, she encouraged me to approach Lifetime TV with the film. It was clear to me that Sherry, always the gracious person she is, and another "giant" along my life journey, had opened a door for me at Lifetime, the largest cable TV network in the world.

Jane never thought her film would be distributed; less than 1 percent of all films made ever are. It is a difficult, wretched business. All she wanted to do was to direct *What Matters Most*, with our daughter Polly in the lead—and she did just that, and more. She had no expectations of distribution. But I always thought differently. I guess it's my marketing mentality.

Chateau Wally Films and *What Matters Most* was a passion of personal intent, but certainly a one-off project. Jane was battling breast cancer and desperately wanted to direct this film, even if she ultimately did not survive the disease. I was not cut out to be a moviemaker, nor am I passionate about any of the aspects of making films. However, I was intensely passionate about seeing my wife reach her dream before she lost her battle with breast cancer.

Although it was a short-lived "Life No. 4," the film went on to win numerous awards at international film festivals, including Best Film, Most Promising New Actress, and Best Director at premiere festivals such as The New York International Independent Film & Video Festival, the Los Angeles Win Femme Festival, the Portland Festival of World Cinema, and the Texas Independent Film Festival, among several others. I also hired Alyson Dutch of Brown & Dutch, talented event managers from Malibu, California, to arrange a ten-major-city tour of the film in the United States as a means to raise funds and awareness for breast cancer. It was a very successful undertaking and probably contributed to the ultimate success of *What Matters Most.*

Although few films made ever receive distribution, *What Matters Most* was fortunately licensed to Lifetime Entertainment. The film became one of Lifetime's most popular movies so they renewed their contract. And today, *What Matters Most* is licensed in more than fifty countries worldwide. *Had we not elected to do the film ourselves, Jane would not have lived long enough to make the film.* What Matters Most *was the result of a critical decision created at a crossroads.* It was a decision fueled by deep thought, passion, and personal commitment. Jane was the "giant" who asked the right question at the right time, "Why don't we make this movie ourselves?" And Sherry Lansing was the "giant" who helped it materialize at Lifetime Television. It became a destiny based on several key synchronizations, or as Deepak Chopra likes to say, "a synchrodestiny."

For quite some time, I held up in our estate in Ojai, California, writing, mountain climbing, and just trying to figure out where to go next with my life. It was a very difficult period. I had two grown daughters, three grandchildren, and although there were several interesting offers to assume the CEO position at technology startups, I really did not want to return to building new enterprises in Silicon Valley. Been there, done that, and the passion was just not there to do it again. I meditated and prayed daily on what to do next. And mostly, I meditated to relieve the relentless anxiety and depression I had suffered since Jane's death.

Life No. 5—Holistic Hotelier

On January 9, 2002, at 1:30 p.m., Pacific Standard Time, my prayers were answered in a way I had never anticipated when an incredibly talented and beautiful "giant" arrived at my home in Ojai, and I began what would be my entree into "Life No. 5." David Walker, a friend and film producer from San Marino, California, asked if he could visit my home, Château Wally. The home was so named because it was built in 1926 for the Forbes family[13] by well-known American architect, Wallace Neff. Neff had built homes for many of the Hollywood celebrities during the Golden Age of film, including Mary Pickford, Groucho Marx, Carey Grant, and Douglas Fairbanks, among others. Today, Wallace Neff homes are owned by the likes of Jennifer Aniston, Reese Witherspoon, Diane Keaton, Madonna, and Guy Ritchie. Jane and I had restored the home to its natural beauty and David had mentioned that his wife, Iveta, loved to visit heritage properties.

When David and Iveta arrived, I met them at the long circular drive that approached the entrance to my home in Ojai's verdant East End. After a cordial hello, I noticed a tall, statuesque, strikingly-beautiful blonc exit from the back of their car. I completely lost my bearings and found myself attracted to her immediately. Her name was Inez Šipulova. She was Iveta's close friend and was visiting from Prague in the Czech Republic. I had no intention of marrying again, or for that matter, even starting a relationship with another woman, but Inez captured my spirit immediately. After Jane's death I became one of the most eligible bachelors from Ojai to Santa Barbara. But I had no interest. I rejected all invitations to parties, dances, teas, you name it. I just wanted to be alone to think and meditate on where to go next with my life, as I journeyed through the various stages of mourning over Jane's death.

However, this time it was just like that scene in the movie *The Godfather* when Michael Corleone, hiding in Sicily from the U.S. authorities, sees and immediately falls in love with the breathtakingly beautiful Apollonia. In Sicilian dialect we like to say he was hit with "fulminare," a thunderbolt! And boy, was I hit—hard! I invited Inez to dinner the next evening. It was a wonderful and engaging experience. I found her not only young, beautiful, and personable, but also intelligent beyond her years. Yes, she is twenty-six years younger than I. Inez unfortunately had to return to Prague in a few days. So I caught the very first flight I could get to Prague, and we have been together ever since. I fell deeply in love with Inez, then with Prague, and finally with a project that she was in the process of developing. After receiving her master's degree in economics and international business in 1988, Inez went to work for several months in Japan, not to Tokyo, but to Kyushu, that country's southernmost island. This was a brave move. Very few people spoke English there, and they were all nearly a meter shorter than she! Inez is tall, so it must have been quite a sight to see her ride a crowded Japanese subway train. But she was interested—and still is—in Asian culture. She persisted, learned some Japanese, and before long had private use of the president's car and driver at the company where she worked.

In 1989, shortly after her return to Prague, what was then Czechoslovakia went through the famous peaceful "Velvet Revolution" and the fall of communism. The country subsequently divided into two countries, the Czech Republic and the Slovak Republic, or Slovakia. There were numerous business opportunities for graduates who could speak a foreign language, especially English. Inez, being quite fluent in a number of languages including English, quickly found an opportunity which led to her becoming Managing Director of a premier heritage restoration and development company. She worked intensely to build the company, and among her many accomplishments, she converted an old, worn-down Vietnamese market in Prague into an upscale Western style shopping center, the first one in the Czech and Slovak Republics and probably in all of Central and Eastern Europe. It won numerous international awards. Although internationally recognized in her field, Inez eventually decided that she would take a break from her eighty-hour-per-week intense effort and travel the world to decide on a job that was more connected to her spirit and core values.

At about the same time, David and Iveta Walker were considering setting up a non-profit foundation, and Iveta, having Slovak roots as Inez does, asked Inez if she would look for a castle to become home to their foundation. Inez drew a one-hour-drive circle on the map around Prague and visited all of the castles that were potentially for sale. She came across Chateau Mcely in the three-hundred-person village of Mcely (sounds like "meh-selly"). It was dilapidated and in terrible condition, but Inez felt a very special energy there. When she approached the castle entrance for the first time it was overgrown with weeds and broken branches, and she was met by a part-time caretaker. He stared into her eyes with intent and calmly and mystically inquired, "Where have you been all these years? We have been waiting for you." It was a truly mystical moment as chills ran through her entire body.

It was the only castle located high on a hill, surrounded by a beautiful forest, with no industry in sight, only lush vegetable farms. She sent a picture of the castle to Iveta, who immediately rejected the possibility of buying it, perhaps because she could not feel what Inez felt, and most probably because it was in such a wretched state.

About six months before we met, Inez bought the castle herself. She had never set out to do so, but there was something tugging at her heart strings that said, "Buy me!" She had preliminary plans to make it into a special retreat where people could go to experience a "higher level of consciousness." She is fond of quoting Albert Einstein who said, "Problems cannot be solved at the same level of consciousness at which they were created."

We decided to work on this project together as business partners. Our dream to do so materialized with the help of Inez, this new and very special "giant" in my life. She applied to the European Union for funds to help with the restoration. Although only a small percentage of the overall investment, when we received positive confirmation from the EU we decided—let's do it! Just as in committing to shoot the movie, *What Matters Most*, this was a high-risk project. In fact we were advised by numerous people in the hospitality business that it would be difficult to attract people to stay in a luxury chateau located in the forest and not in Prague proper. In a sense, it would have to become a highly desirable destination on its own. It had never been done before in either the Czech or Slovak Republics. But when the European Union came through with funding, we decided to do it. And we never looked back.

To be clear, Inez was and still is the primary visionary behind what was to become an internationally recognized property, and arguably the Czech Republic's most popular castle retreat. Within three years of meeting, we married, gave birth to little Julia, completely renovated the castle and opened for business in September 2006. Our journey through renovation and opening the Chateau Mcely, a seventeenth century chateau and former residence of the Thurn-Taxis aristocracy,[14] is documented in a heartfelt book written by Inez[15] and in a documentary film.[16] The film runs continuously on one of the TV channels in each of the chateau's room.

Within a couple of years, the chateau became recognized as one of the most exclusive venues in Central and Eastern Europe for conferences, corporate events, weddings, training, and romantic getaways. We became members of Small Luxury Hotels of the World (SLH), and soon received a number of prestigious accolades.[17] Chateau Mcely was awarded first place in 2006 as the *Best Hotel Project in the Czech Republic*. In 2007 it was designated by the European Union as *the only GREEN 5-Star hotel in Central and Eastern Europe*, and in 2008 Chateau Mcely won the World Travel Award as *The World's Leading Green Hotel*, proving that luxury and a respect for nature need not be mutually exclusive. Our team, Inez, and I were more than grateful and pleased when luxury magazine *Dolce Vita* named Chateau Mcely "The Best Boutique Hotel in the Czech Republic."

It was the outcome of this article that prompted us to change our operating strategy. We originally intended Chateau Mcely to be an event center for weddings and perhaps corporate events. We would live there full-time and maintain a small core group of employees, expanding our core with part-time help using students from a nearby hotel school whenever an event was booked. When the editor of *Dolce Vita* visited the castle, he fell in love with it and instead of just a few lines of coverage he published a seven-page article containing numerous color photos.

After publication we were inundated by requests to stay at our "hotel." So, after much thought and consideration, and not unlike the change in strategy we had made at Catalytica when we purchased the world-class pharmaceutical plant in North Carolina, Inez and I decided to respond to the market. We enlarged our staff as necessary and focused our energy and passion on becoming one of the top hotel spas and forest retreats in Central and Eastern Europe.

Under Inez's direction Chateau Mcely was meticulously renovated to its original neoclassical architecture, yet unobtrusively fitted with all of the conveniences of modern technology—broad band and Wi-Fi throughout, IP telephony, videoconferencing, and plasma TV. Visitors seem to thoroughly enjoy the ambiance of the chateau's "spirit in nature" venue. After a scenic hike in the adjacent six hundred-hectare game park, they often go for a swim in a naturally-cleansed bio-lake, partake in a specially-prepared royal picnic along the water, relax in our lakeside sauna and Jacuzzi, and then experience the beauty of body meets spirit in the chateau's spa with one of its specially-designed therapies. Spa products are prepared in the chateau laboratory from locally grown herbs in accordance with ancient alchemical formulae and procedures.

The castle has twenty-three custom suites and rooms, each individually decorated. It sleeps fifty-five people. Unique gourmet dishes from its Piano Nobile Restaurant and fine wines are offered by a talented international chef. In 2010, 2011, and 2012 it was named one of the top ten restaurants in the Czech Republic. The décor, services, activities, and location provide a holistic environment that arguably meets Einstein's criteria for dealing with challenging issues through a balance of body, mind, and spirit.[18] Chateau Mcely's promise to its list of international clients such as Young Presidents Organization (YPO), Aspen Institute, PricewaterhouseCoopers, Google,

Lamborghini, Brown-Forman, Cisco Systems, Christian Dior, DHL, the European Union, Pfizer, and many others is consistently clear and focused: *"Our vision is to make a difference in the world by making a difference in yours."*

Inez and I did not renovate Chateau Mcely simply to be in the hotel, spa, and restaurant businesses. Our strategy from the very outset was to create a "place" where the nexus and balance of body, mind, and spirit occur so naturally and seamlessly that it need not even be discussed or orchestrated. The "place" automatically produces highly desirable results. We have proven that Chateau Mcely can do just that as a successful commercial enterprise. If you page through the more than 1,000 pages in our current guestbook or read the comments on TripAdvisor,[19] you can see that a broad international demographic spectrum of guests seems to say the same thing over and over again, but in different words: "What incredible service; what marvelous food; a spa like no other; what a special place; I have felt something here that I have not experienced elsewhere."

There are many fascinating stories throughout Chateau Mcely's long history; some are perhaps mythical, some would even say mystical. Most allude to the castle's special energy. There have been castles at this location since the fourteenth century and Celtic ruins dating back a few thousand years were discovered nearby several years ago. In our short experience since opening in 2006, we too have seen the unfolding of a number of interesting stories. One touching event occurred with our very first guests, an international meeting of the Young Presidents' Organization (YPO). The members were all bright CEOs from a number of countries throughout the world. One of them was a young lady who is an investment banker in South Africa, where she lives as a single mom with her nine-year-old daughter.

Because she was going to be gone for some time on international travel, she bought her daughter a small puppy and told her not to let the puppy out of the compound where they live. At the time there were still significant remnants of Apartheid in their neighborhood. Our guest had been at Chateau Mcely for only a few hours when she received a call from her daughter in South Africa crying desperately that the puppy had escaped through the gate. It was so serious that the young banker was considering returning to South Africa in the morning to comfort her daughter.

That evening, as she dressed for dinner in her room, she noticed a statue of the Virgin Mary in our gardens. It was placed there to commemorate the famous Marian apparitions of the Virgin Mary to three young Mcely children on our property in 1849, nine years before she is said to have appeared to fourteen-year-old Bernadette Soubirous in Lourdes, France. As our guest looked down at the statue, she thought aloud in desperation, "Look, Mary, I'm Jewish and I don't know much about you and your apparition here at Chateau Mcely, but if there is anything you can do for my little girl, I would be deeply grateful." That evening she went to sleep, fully intending to book a return flight to South Africa in the morning. She was awakened at 3:30 a.m. by her daughter, who was as jubilant as can be. The security guard had found her puppy.

As part of our body-mind-spirit strategy, we recently launched Mcely Bouquet,[20] a collection of totally-natural skincare and spa products. These products were developed over a two-year period by Inez who worked closely with a cosmetic chemist, using ancient alchemical techniques. She has had a lifelong interest in natural cosmetics and aromatherapy. We set up a laboratory at Chateau Mcely for developing our products and for their manufacture. Initial response from the market has been very favorable, so we expect this effort to continue as an important part of our focus in the realm of body and spirit.

Inspired by the *Eloise* books written in the mid-1950s by Kay Thompson about a precocious little girl who lives at the Plaza Hotel in Manhattan, Inez is currently completing a book entitled *Nely, Princess of Mcely*.[21] The pictures in the book are beautifully drawn by a local Czech artist. The stories portray the imagination and actual games played in the castle and created by our six-year-old Julia. All of the *Eloise* books begin with, "I am Eloise. I am six. I am a city child. I live at the Plaza." The Nely books have a similar sense, but are based on real exploits by a real six-year-old in a real castle. Inez is also working with local artisans to offer a number of Nely products, and is in the process of a completing a renovated suite at Chateau Mcely just for little princesses.

An integral part of our "mind" strategy has been to bring to Chateau Mcely recognized world experts who can teach and influence high-level corporate and political leaders to foster effective addressing of critical global issues such as climate change, energy security, and healthcare. The fundamental point here is creating a new kind of leadership—Conscious or inspired leadership—enlightened leaders, who naturally, unpresumptuously, and compassionately inspire those around them, and who are driven to serve all of their stakeholders, through their commitment to the "3-P Bottom Line"—People, Planet, Profit.

In doing so, the goal is to create inspiring visions, missions, and values that permeate and motivate every individual in their organization to create products and services that make this a better world. We are now implementing this next step of our strategy—bringing talented and proven experts in leadership and related areas to Chateau Mcely to help us make an even greater difference in the world. We call this the *Chateau Mcely Forum*™.[22] Our first program was successfully launched in June 2011 as *Leadership for Life.*[23] We brought to Prague and to Chateau Mcely Dr. Lance Secretan, a former CEO of Manpower Inc. and a world leader and the architect of the principles of Inspirational Leadership®.[24] His presence has had multiple positive impacts within the Czech Republic, and we continue to invite great thinkers such as Lance to Prague. Similar programs have followed and continue on a regular basis.

We think programs such as those offered by Chateau Mcely Forum are important to stimulate thinking as to how our world can safely and expeditiously transition to a new paradigm, a new way of "being." The current paradigm based on excessive utilization of resources without regard to the impact on the environment and on the lives of others, may have worked since the inception of the industrial revolution, but it is now a very dangerous trajectory for the future of humanity.

* * *

There were a number of other critical crossroads in my life, junctures that determined my degree of personal fulfillment, my true meaning in life, my destiny. We all have them. Recognizing these decision points and taking appropriate action, guided by a "giant" who supports your emotional, spiritual, and intellectual growth is the secret to a meaningful life and a successful business.

As I will work diligently to show you in the pages that follow, once you determine that special skill that you were born with and you connect it with a positive need in the world, you will have found your life purpose. You will find that the passion you generate from this discovery will create incredible levels of emotional and physical energy. You will then have the wherewithal to proceed and persist with continual success and fulfillment along the way—not just as a final goal. From that point all that is required is tenacity, good judgment based on the counsel of the giants you meet along the way, and dedicated effort. You don't have to be gifted with a special set of genes or a super high IQ. *Everyone* is capable of achieving the success and happiness of a balanced life.

So this has been my professional life—so far! I am sometimes asked "How many more professional lives will you have?" or "What will the next one be?" I have no idea. My journey so far has been a gift beyond all my expectations. I am deeply grateful. And I would be more than happy to stay with No. 5; but I always keep my senses open to the universe and the giants I may meet along the way. You never know!

I am also asked quite often, "If you could go back in time, what would you change?" I must say that I am so satisfied with my current state in life that I would be hesitant to change anything, even the disappointments, lest it alter my much fulfilled overall existence. Yes, it is true that I've had my share of challenges. Jane's death is certainly a vivid example. But in retrospect and after managing my transition to a new life, I can look back and say that the universe granted me the most incredible opportunity to grow with and love the two most magnificent women I have ever met. My love for Inez is as deep as I can fathom, and she has melded us even closer into "oneness" by giving birth to our bright, vibrant, and spirited young daughter Julia, the youngest of my three princesses—Doreen (age forty-six), Polly (age thirty-six), and Julia (age six). I am reminded constantly by these three lovely ladies that I must stay healthy and vital if I am to dance at Julia's wedding!

I think you have to learn to manage the "mountains-of-challenge" in life to arrive at the "verdant-valleys-of-fulfillment." And if you do it well, the rewards are remarkable. No one gets a free ride. And every stage in life builds on previous experiences. The Buddhists got it right—that's just karma! I have never said that my successes happened *despite* the challenges I faced in life; rather, I am convinced that they happened *because* of these challenges. Surmounting obstacles has a way of teaching us truths we might never have uncovered, and opening doors that might never have been opened for us.

As you travel through this book, my hope is that for each chapter you read you will get at least one solid idea of value, something you can hang on to, something that touches your very heart and soul, something that will make a positive difference in your life.

PART II

Creating a Fulfilling Life

Unleash Purpose & Passion
Stimulate Creativity & Innovation
Find True Success & Happiness

CHAPTER 2

Finding Your Purpose and Passion

You have succeeded in discovering your Personal Legend ... It's what you have always wanted to accomplish ... Everyone, when they are young, knows what their Personal Legend is.[25]

—Paulo Coelho

KEY CONCEPTS

◆ It is *never* too late to find your *true* purpose and passion in life.

◆ The first step is an honest answer to each of *four provocative questions*.

◆ The second step is to develop an action plan that follows from your answers and courageously pursue it.

You are eminently capable of finding that special part of your body, mind, and spirit that distinguishes you from all others in your professional and personal circles—that unique "something" which gives you sheer pleasure and has the potential to generate great value for both you and the world.

Individuals Have a Unique Purpose and Passion

That "something" is nothing less than your *true* purpose and passion in life. Everyone has it. We are born with it. It's your very essence, your core. The alchemists of old called it the "Fifth Element," your "Quintessence." It's the real you, not what you or someone else *thinks* you should be, but—deep down—what you have always wanted to be—*what you were born to be*!

Most of us innately "know" what it is when we are quite young, but for many of us, the machinations and rapid momentum of our modern technological world are a distraction and can push us on to another track—one that is often unsatisfying and unproductive. Your parents always wanted you to be a doctor, or a lawyer, or to fall in line and follow the family business. And so, you did. But is that what you really wanted to do? My friend and long-time business partner, Ricardo Levy, provides insight on this point in his book *Letters to a Young Entrepreneur,*[26] where he quotes a salient comment by Glenda Grunzweig in her book *The Geography of Love:*[27] "What you dream of yourself at age fourteen reflects your purest wish."

Or possibly there is a recording that has echoed over and over again in your mind since childhood, something like, "Everyone knows that a degree in business is the best way to a high-paying job and financial freedom. And for goodness sake, forget about your interest and special capabilities in the arts or music or sports. Do you want to be a pauper all of your life?" Many people end up pursuing "practical" professions, not ones that are based on their innate strengths, capabilities, and deep interest. Here, "practical" equates to a means to money, status, and power. This has been the definition of a practical profession for more than three centuries.

Is it any wonder that recent studies show that only about 20 percent of employees are happy with their jobs?[28] And as for so-called "successful" business people, less than 20 percent have truly satisfying marriages and close relationships.[29] More often than not, your true interests and capabilities, if properly pursued, have the highest probability of providing personal satisfaction and also in making a positive impact on the world around you.

Years ago, when I worked at Exxon as a research director, I had a colleague who was a brilliant and successful scientist. For quite some time, conditioned and influenced by people around him, he *thought* that he should be a manager. "I want to move into management and administration. I've done the science stuff. It's time for me to move *up* in the world," he would proclaim—"Up" because it is generally and correctly perceived that managers have greater responsibility for personnel and receive higher pay than scientists do.

When finally placed in that position, he became utterly distraught and asked management to send him back to the lab. Higher pay and greater power completely lost their appeal to him. When they acquiesced, he finally recognized his true sense of purpose and passion. He was genuinely happy! In his rediscovered sense of purpose and fulfillment he continued to make creative and successful technological contributions for which he was handsomely rewarded by Exxon!

It is my conviction and personal experience that *if you earnestly uncover and follow your innate purpose and passion and build your life around them, you are much more capable of creating both a successful and a balanced life and the enriched relationships that flow from success based on this vital sense of balance. I also discovered that this new-found purpose, passion, and sense of balance usually unfolds creative approaches to tough challenges and, even for the most "ordinary" pursuits, can result in significant emotional and financial returns.*

In fact, it is nearly impossible to have a truly successful life without the balance that, if truth be known, is what your soul really yearns for in the first place. If you have lost sight of your purpose and passion in life, have no fear—you can recapture it! Forget the "only-one-job" myth, created during a long-gone age when it was the norm to follow a single profession for your entire life and receive a gold watch at retirement. It is never too late to change—under almost any set of circumstances. It does, however, require courage, commitment, and a true internal sense that you can uncover a reasonable strategy that will help you make the transition, successfully. The great thing about this process is that once you re-identify and recapture your true life purpose, the passion created just in that step alone often provides all of the motivation, courage, and energy you will need to make the change.

The Power of Four Questions

I have a friend who is a psychologist, a teacher, a best-selling author, and over the years from time to time has been my personal advisor. His name is Dr. Gay Hendricks and he has written numerous books, some of which have appeared on the *New York Times* Best Seller list. Long ago, he gave me a single piece of paper on which were written four provocative questions. Contemplating those questions helped me realize how, quite early on, I had actually focused on capabilities that are unique to me. I have been fortunate to have parents, teachers, and friends who were supportive of my two chosen diverse interests—entertainment and technology—even when it meant transitioning from one professional "life" to another.

Gay's structure and wisdom helped me to see the power of his method and how it could help others. These four questions are easy to ask, but quite challenging to answer. However, in doing so, you can achieve significant insight into your capabilities and match them with your desire for a positive lifelong journey. Gay discusses his approach in his book entitled *Making the Big Leap*.[30] I found his questions so profound that I would like to share them together with my own personal answers. But first a few remarks about the process.

To achieve best results with this inquiry requires a concerted, consistent, and focused effort, but the outcome is more than worthwhile. After all, it is *your* life! When contemplating these questions you might sit comfortably in a quiet place, for example, in the wilds of nature, at the seaside, on a mountain, or perhaps simply in a quiet place at your home—wherever you feel safe, quiet, meditative, and inspired. If you meditate daily, you will find the process to be significantly easier, especially when contemplating these questions immediately before meditation and letting them sink into and percolate within your subconscious.

In asking these questions you must be totally honest, and not provide answers that your parents, loved ones, a teacher, or your boss might like to hear. Don't be frustrated if the answers don't come immediately—they almost never do—but in time you will move into the answers. Be patien and tenacious. The more often you practice this meditative process, the sooner you will have your answers. Followed diligently and with commitment this process always works.

Answers to these four questions must come from deep within your soul. The answers should be the absolute truth and not—as was the case for my scientist friend at Exxon—what you think they should be based on the prejudice or predisposition of others. Also, there is no room for modesty in this undertaking. Don't worry about being egocentric; you are only speaking to yourself. And besides, you're looking at that part of you which is exciting and probably more adept than many of those around you!

And please, don't concern yourself with making lots of money. It will just confuse the process. Sure, as Abraham Maslow[31] and Viktor Frankl[32] professed, you must make enough money to satisfy your so-called basic "hygienic" needs, but anything after that is usually a measure of your professional "progress." Besides, there are literally hundreds of examples which show that financial success often follows from pursuit of your purpose and passion in life. I can personally attest to this. Every professional pursuit I have followed was based on my personal capabilities, predilections, and passion. And each time I achieved more emotional and financial success than I might ever have imagined at the outset.

To begin the process, I urge you to think back to your youth as well as your current stage in life and focus on those things that interest you above all others. It is likely they continually captured your interest as a youth. When you were young—somewhere between the ages of five and fifteen—they were perhaps expressed in an unusual manner—you knew exactly what you were good at and what area of professional pursuit was best for you and for the world around you.

Studies have shown that the prime reason for this is that children in this age range want essentially two fundamental things in their lives:[33] they want to be with their friends and they want to feel good about themselves in their innate drive for high self-esteem. The best way for them to accomplish both of these objectives is to do what they are passionate about and what they are really good at. Note that *at this stage in their lives they are not distracted by pursuits that promise loads of money or power and prestige.* They want their peers to like them, and they want to love what they do. So mechanically-adept children impress their friends by what they can fix and build. Artistically well-endowed children wow themselves and others with their skills in the arts, budding super athletes outperform their competition on the playing field, and so on. Nearly all children in this age range understand clearly what they are good at and what they like to do.

Please understand that being artistically adept or inclined does not mean the child necessarily is destined to become a successful artist in the classical sense. It may mean he or she will express their artistic passions in a related way, perhaps as an architect or an art critic, or commercial designer. Similarly a child competent in sports may be destined to be a sports agent or possibly open a sporting goods store. The range of possibilities is enormous.

I'll share a story with you to illustrate what I mean about discovering your professional interest as a child. Starting when she was just three years old, my daughter Julia, who is currently six years old, began to be captivated by just about any living organism. She has no fear of insects or of just about any animal. I had to teach her not to pick up bees and spiders, which she reluctantly obeys, although she has been stung three times! Perched on a chair at my desk and glued to one of my vintage microscopes, Julia can study the dance of bacteria and other microorganisms for hours on end.

Once at the Prague Zoo she was bitten quite hard feeding a goat in the petting arena. But that did not stop her. She was back feeding the same animals a week later. If you ask her what she wants to do when she grows up, she immediately responds, "a veterinarian!" I have no idea if that's the journey she will follow, but I will be absolutely surprised if her chosen profession does not have some biological component in it. Julia is only six years old, yet she likely knows the future direction of her professional life. Of course she doesn't think of it this way at this point in her life, but someday, she likely will.

The best thing that my wife and I can do is continuously expose Julia to a range of possibilities through her toys, games, travel, entertainment, and discussions. At the right point in time, an "aha" moment will release her passion and focus it like a laser on a future possible profession.

If you are not happy with the current state of affairs in your professional life, your answers to the four questions I will pose below may not have anything to do with what you studied in school or what you do in your current job. They could reflect your special ability in athletics, music, photography, art, mechanics, or some other area. And remember, just because certain external influences drove you to become, for example, a lawyer or a banker, does not mean that you must continue working at those professions for the rest of your life. After you have been in one position for some years, making a change always looks more serious and challenging than it actually turns out to be. Don't talk yourself out of trying. Don't get stuck!

My Answers to the Four Questions

I can best exemplify how this process works by applying these questions to my own personal and professional predispositions. So please bear with me as I share with you my responses to the four questions. To put my answers in perspective, I must first remind you of a few things about my history.

As presented in some detail in chapter 1, to date, I have "lived" five professional lives. Early on, I was a singer and musician and performer and traveled with a group called the *Royal Teens* which had several successful recordings during the 1950s and 1960s. Subsequently, I was educated in chemistry and physics and then in business. After several years as a Director of R&D for Exxon, I spent much of my professional career in Silicon Valley, founding and building companies focused in low-cost, environmentally-sustainable technologies. Eventually, I returned to entertainment and founded a film company, which produced and distributed worldwide a feature film entitled *What Matters Most*. More recently, I have worked with my wife and business partner, Inez, who the year before we met purchased Chateau Mcely, a dilapidated Czech castle. Together we renovated and restored it to a luxury hotel, restaurant, spa, and forest retreat.

Chateau Mcely Forum® attracts wise thinkers from around the world to teach a new kind of leadership—a leadership that is effective in dealing transparently with critical crises such as economic collapse, energy security, and climate change.

From this summary, you will probably observe that entrepreneurial connections occurred throughout my life at the interface of technology and entertainment, both connected by the link of business and entrepreneurship. I will elaborate on this point after I disclose my answers to Gay Hendricks'[34] four questions.

Here are the Four Questions and my respective answers:

1. **What do I most love to do, so much so that time passes incredibly quickly?**

   I love to entertain and to teach people important concepts of value that I have learned throughout my life, concepts that have the potential to bring about major positive change. I am particularly drawn to the connections between technology, business, entertainment, and the needs of humanity. I am interested and experienced in the art of inspiring people in business to achieve challenging goals.

   As described in some detail in the first chapter, as a young boy *several key events* foreshadowed *my lifelong purpose, passion, and journey*, and set the stage for the rest of my professional career in science, technology, entertainment, and writing.

   The first of these events occurred during my eighth Christmas when I received a chemistry set. As described previously, after experimenting my way through the typical shenanigans of making stink bombs and fireworks, I became so inspired by the neat "products" I could make that I set up a lab in the basement of my parents home, and there I "manufactured" cosmetics, cleaners, inks, adhesives—you name it—and sold them door to door in our neighborhood. What thrilled me most was not just the money I made, but also the fact that someone was willing to pay for my "products"—an indication that I brought value that made a positive difference to the customer. This formed the basis for my career as a technical entrepreneur and my dedication to the innovation process.

   The second event came about because of my need to work at a young age. Because I am the oldest of ten children and was raised in a family of very modest means, I worked when I was a young boy to support both me and my family. Growing up in the 1950s in New Jersey, across the river from Manhattan—entertainment capital of the world—and because of my natural predilection for modern music and entertainment, I fell in love with rock and roll music. Rather than brave the cold Jersey winters as a paper boy to earn money, I took piano lessons so that I could form a band to do something I was passionate about—playing rock and roll music— and working indoors! This led to my career in entertainment.

The third event presaged my future as a writer. A birthday gift from my parents of a child's typewriter and later a small printing press inspired me to write and "publish" short stories and a neighborhood newspaper, each issue having "paid" advertisements for local merchants. "Paid" usually meant a chocolate candy bar. Over the years, my writing of numerous papers, articles, and books sprung forth from that little typewriter and printing press.

2. **What work do I do or have I done in the past that I do not consider work?**

I have always enjoyed speaking (teaching), writing, and entertaining (singing)—especially for the benefit of others.

As an example of combining my experiences in technology, business, and entertainment to benefit others, I was recently invited to give a presentation to several hundred college students in Slovakia. They were primarily first- and second-year students getting prepared to declare their major field of study. The organizers asked me to speak on finding personal and professional fulfillment, and because of my past life in entertainment and rock and roll music, they requested that I close with a song, which I did—an Elvis Presley medley.[35]

I was certainly gratified by the standing ovation when I finished my performance, but I was more moved by the conversation afterwards and the genuine interest and commitment of these young students to find their fundamental strengths, to then build on these skills and connect them with an important need in the world, and thereby to make it a better place in which to live.

I continue to pursue these joys by writing business and technical articles and books. I find enough time to do a few "Oldies" concerts each year and donate my compensation to charity. Since "charity begins at home," I continue to sing on stage at Chateau Mcely for special occasions, such as our New Year's Eve Gala event. If I wanted or had to, I am confident that I could still make a living as a professional entertainer.

3. **What could I do that would create the greatest value for the world around me, as well as the greatest personal satisfaction for the amount of time spent?**

With my deep sense of vision and mission, I could bring together and inspire talented people—much more talented than I—who are capable of having a positive impact on critical issues facing humanity by the effective interface of business, entertainment, and technology.

It was this passion that helped me play a leadership role in founding and building successful businesses in the United States and now in Europe. Catalytica Energy Systems developed the world's first clean catalytic combustion system for generating power and electricity. Catalytica Pharmaceuticals, which created cost-effective, environmentally-sustainable technologies for the manufacture of drugs, was Silicon Valley's fastest growing company for two consecutive years and a global leader in pharmaceuticals manufacturing. It grew in less than five years from essentially nothing to a public company valued at over $1 billion. We manufactured some of the world's most important drugs for the major pharmaceutical companies.

All of this occurred successfully because my business partner Ricardo Levy and I were able to hire and inspire absolutely brilliant, capable people—people with much more talent in their chosen field than either Ricardo or I had. We saw our primary job as a commitment and dedicated effort to support and inspire these talented individuals. And we loved it! Our deepest joy flowed from the success of the entire team.

4. **What is my unique ability, the skill or skills which if truly actualized could provide significant benefits to the organization for which I work, to the world, and to me?**

I have a personal "presence" that is fostered by my knowledge of and experience in technology, entertainment, and business. This "presence" quickly connects with people. My multidisciplinary background often brings great value.

It was this "presence" which enticed record producer Leo Rodgers to sign me to his recording company and to reform the Royal Teens. It was the same "presence" that enabled me to become the

youngest research director at Exxon's Corporate Research Laboratory, leading a group of brilliant scientists and engineers, most of
whom were much more intelligent than I.

To give an example of this, I offer a short story. When my partners and I were raising venture capital for the first time, we sought a
valuation for our fledgling company that was 20 percent higher than
that proposed by the Mayfield Fund, the lead venture group. Shortly
before we were to finalize our negotiations, Ricardo Levy and I met
with Jim Blair, the managing director of a venture capital firm that
represented the Rothschild Fund from the United Kingdom. They
were interested in putting money into our company. During our
dinner with them Ricardo told Jim about my prior career in music.
He suddenly exclaimed, "Now I know why you look so familiar, I
saw you several times some years ago on Dick Clark's American
Bandstand TV Show. That's just fantastic! Would you be willing
to sing for our annual venture capitalist party?" Shortly after that
dinner, his company contributed 50 percent of our initial venture
funding and both venture groups agreed to our higher valuation.

* * *

I want to emphasize strongly that my successes were absolutely NOT a
consequence of a high level of innate capabilities. Yes, I consider myself to
have a reasonable high intelligence (IQ) and a decent level of emotional
intelligence (EQ). However, over the years I have met numerous men and
women with much greater innate capabilities and higher levels of IQ and
EQ, many of whom never achieved their goals in life or reached any reasonable level of self-fulfillment. This was usually because they had not
discovered and pursued their true life purpose and passion. I believe that
my successes followed the "80-20" rule. Twenty percent was due to my
innate strengths, capabilities, and native intelligence; but the lion's share—
80 percent, or so—was definitely based on my early discovery of my fundamental essence, my life purpose, that was fueled by the energy of passion
and guided by the "giants" in my life. I made lots of mistakes along the way,
but none that could not be overcome by my passion to follow my dream.
You can do the same. I am absolutely sure of it.

It is so unfortunate how many of us underestimate our innate power and potential to make this a better world and in the process to blossom in fulfillment beyond our wildest dreams. Once you get just a taste of the progress you can make along the journey designated by your purpose and passion, you will not be able to turn back. You will feel a deep sense of exhilaration—high levels of both emotional and physical energy—and you will accomplish much more than the humble goals you had previously set for yourself. You will have put a dent in the universe and made this a better world.

Honest answers and an action plan that follows from these answers can make a huge difference in moving you towards goals that make life a much more satisfying, productive, and rewarding journey. Why try to live someone else's dream, even if that dream belongs to your parents, a teacher, or a loved one? It can't be done. And besides, as impossible as it may seem at this very moment, it requires much less effort to follow your own purpose and passion than to become an unhappy "prisoner" trying to live someone else's dream.

CHAPTER 3

CREATING YOUR LIFE PLAN

*"... if one advances confidently in the direction of his dreams,
and endeavors to live the life which he has imagined, he will
meet with a success {that is} unexpected..."*[36]

—HENRY DAVID THOREAU

KEY CONCEPTS

- You can create practical one-year, three-year, and five-year life plans.
- These plans can be your compass and direct your efforts to help you meet your goals in a timely manner.
- First, it is necessary to develop your personal vision, mission, and values.
- Your values can be divided into "Six Spheres for Personal and Professional Growth."
- It is most effective if your goals are based on specific dates for completion.

OKAY, SO NOW YOU KNOW YOUR PURPOSE IN LIFE and you have found your true passion. How do you create a personal plan to make sure that your future unfolds in an effective and manageable way? Some people can do this mentally and never take the time to write down a single goal on paper. Those who do this well are few and far between. I recall only one person during my professional career who did this very effectively. The late Henry Taube was a dear friend, a professor of chemistry at Stanford University, and a part-time employee of Catalytica, Inc., the company I cofounded. Henry was also the recipient of the 1983 Nobel Prize in chemistry. He never wrote down a goal or even a meeting date or time. Yet he was able to manage his personal and professional life with great success. Perhaps it was his photographic memory? Not an easy way to operate for us mere mortals!

Most of us profit immensely from a more rigorous process, wherein we struggle to identify specific meaningful goals. You can do this for a one-year period, but because successful achievement of your one-year goals has clear implication for the years beyond, it is useful to struggle with your best assessment as to where you would like to be in three years and possibly five years, as well. Yes, even three years is a long time, but you will be surprised as to how effective this planning can be in not only guiding your current actions, but actually manifesting those goals you set in your sights—even five years into the future.

Once the process is completed, it is straightforward and not very time-consuming to update and modify the plan on an annual basis. But the first time, the required effort can be significant. *The fundamental point here is that since you first create your reality in your mind, clarity of purpose and pursuit is a very powerful tool for manifesting into your life those things that are most important to you and the goals you seek to achieve.* It has been shown over and over again that there is great and perhaps inexplicable power in "connecting pen to paper" to record your thoughts and hone them down to specific goals and strategies that you feel will lead to a balanced and fulfilled life. Even if the ultimate strategy turns out to be different than you had anticipated, this kind of clarity avoids inefficient distractions and it focuses all of your emotional and physical energy on what you want to achieve in this world.

The First Step

Before coming up with a life plan, it is important to know, internalize, and overtly state your *vision* and *mission* in life. Your *vision* should create a picture in your mind's eye of how you want your world to be. You are looking through a virtual telescope into the future and you are visualizing your world as you would like it to be. Your *mission* should summarize the role you want to play in helping to move your world in that direction. So, your vision is what you *see* and your mission is what you *do* to help make it happen.

For some people, a simple *"Dream"* statement is most motivating and can serve as their combined *vision* and *mission* statements. For example, suppose that your *vision* statement is, "To live in a cleaner, more sustainable world." And let's say that you're an expert in a certain area of information technologies (IT) with a *mission* to use your skills for environmental sustainability. Your *Dream* statement could be "To help create a sustainable future through my skills in IT" or "To dedicate my IT skills for a sustainable future for humanity." The statement should be easy to remember and one that inspires your passion when you think of it or state it to someone else.

Values Are Your Compass

Over the years I have found that it is important that the goals and plan I create are most effective if they are solidly based on my personal values. Therefore, after you clearly understand, embrace, and have internalized your *vision* and *mission* statements, I suggest that you answer the following important question: "What are the core *values* that guide me through life?" These are guidelines and are not necessarily ethically right or wrong; and they certainly are not absolute edicts that are meant to dictate the behavior of all individuals. Rather, they are fundamental truths and beliefs that are important to you.

Your core *values* are intimately connected to your deepest intuition and "tell" you what you are most comfortable with when making decisions or taking action. They are an intimate part of your consciousness and are meant to guide your actions—a kind of internal compass that always points to your personal absolute truth. Some of your core *values* may be "genetic" in the sense that you entered this world with them; and others may be "environmental," developed early on in life, a consequence of your personal relationships and external influences.

The Ignatian Tradition of the Jesuit Order espouses a philosophy that addresses this issue. It maintains that before making a decision you should practice *Discernment*, which involves two concepts: *Consolation* and *Desolation*. In her book *Inner Compass: An Invitation to Ignatian Spirituality*, Margaret Silf provides excellent detailed descriptions of these concepts and the role they play in decision and *Discernment*.[37] The bottom line: Does your decision take you to a higher level of consciousness (*Consolation*), or drive you down the consciousness scale (*Desolation*).[38] Silf points to the following effects:

DESOLATION

- ❖ Turns us in on ourselves
- ❖ Drives us down a spiral deeper into negative feelings
- ❖ Cuts us off from our team and/or our community
- ❖ Makes us want to give up on things that were important to us
- ❖ Takes over our consciousness and crowds out our distant vision
- ❖ Drains us of energy

CONSOLATION

- ❖ Directs our focus outside beyond ourselves
- ❖ Lifts our hearts so that we see the joys and sorrows of others
- ❖ Bonds us more closely to our team and/or community
- ❖ Generates new inspiration, innovation, and creative ideas
- ❖ Restores balance and refreshes our inner vision
- ❖ Shows us where consciousness is active in our lives and where it is leading us
- ❖ Releases new energy in us

You will find that when you violate any of your basic *values,* you create a state of *desolation,* you feel bad, and don't function well regardless of how you may try to rationalize your decision or behavior. Conversely, when your life is in perfect harmony and *balance* with your *values,* you experience *consolation* and you are effective, efficient, and deeply committed in your endeavors. And when these *values* align with your true sense of purpose in life—that fundamental internal core essence that is uniquely yours—intense passion is generated and you are able to pursue your life dream and experience a great level of lasting happiness and fulfillment.

Vision, mission, values, and goals are key components of an effective life plan. Each is very personal, and there is no set "template" for their creation and/or identification. So I thought the best way to convey these concepts is by sharing my own expression of these important elements for well-being and fulfillment. Please consider it simply as an example.

My Vision, Mission, and Dream

The personal *vision* and *mission* statements that I developed over the years are as follows:

> **Vision:** I envision a safe, sustainable, happier future for all through a balance of body, mind, and spirit.

> **Mission:** Through my skills in business, technology, entertainment, and communications, I will establish and grow profitable enterprises and projects which contribute significantly to human sustainability and personal growth and fulfillment.

When I dwell on my personal mission and vision, the inspirational dream that touches my soul is the following:

> **Dream:** Through my gifts in business, technology, and entertainment, I contribute to a more conscious and just humanity that embraces world peace and creates a sustainable future for our children.

Six Spheres for Personal and Professional Growth

Many years ago, I found it helpful to divide my values into what I call "Six Spheres for Personal and Professional Growth." Each of these spheres affects the way I function. I will share with you my personal plan that I updated at the end of 2004 for the years 2005–2010. I have picked this period of time because more than five years have subsequently passed since creating this plan, and as you read through this book, you will notice that most of my actions were effective in achieving my goals. This process really works!

I wrote down my values some years ago, and they have not changed significantly over time; generally, values don't. Only specific goals that I set for one, three, and five-year periods change with time. Here is a summary of my personal values.

1. PROFESSIONAL SPHERE VALUES

What is the underlying principle that guides all of my professional efforts? After much thought, I formulated the following basic value for my professional life:

I channel my professional energies into building profitable enterprises that address my vision and mission and are based on a culture that fosters the personal and professional growth of all participants. These enterprises market products and/or services that help advance our quality of life.

2. FINANCIAL SPHERE VALUES

How important is money to me and how will I use it? My value for this sphere is as follows:

I increase our family wealth as a means to accomplish our goals, but not for aberrant and excessive collection of material things or ego satisfaction.

3. RELATIONSHIP SPHERE VALUES

How important are family, friends, and the community, and where do they fit in my scheme of things? I have been guided by this value:

I take the lead in strengthening family ties, developing new friend-ships, and building on my current relationships. Through my talents in entrepreneurship, communication, technology, leadership, and entertainment, I contribute financially and in personal time to societal needs that I feel will make this a better world.

4. SPIRITUAL SPHERE VALUES

What is sacred to me and how does this generally manifest itself in my life? My guiding principle has been based on the following value:

I diligently study the spiritual and scientific nature of consciousness as a means of seeking answers or at least some understanding to the fundamental questions of life and the universe—Who am I? Where did I come from? What is my purpose? Where, if anywhere, will I "go" after I die?

5. HEALTH SPHERE VALUES

How important is my health and vitality and what do I do about it? My actions are guided by:

I exercise daily to maintain a healthy body and mind. I continuously envision myself as a healthy individual and seek new ways to build my spiritual, emotional, and physical vitality.

6. KNOWLEDGE SPHERE VALUES

How important is past, present, and future knowledge to me and what do I do about it? My commitment to acquiring knowledge is as follows:

I continually develop my mind and spirit through leadership and learning. I build on my strengths and address areas in which I seek improvement. I enhance my being through courses, reading, travel, learning, self-reflection, and asking for feedback from family, friends, and fellow workers. I integrate this feedback and learning into building and honing my persona, my mind, my psyche, and my spirit.

As was the case in answering the four questions in chapter 2, it is important that you provide truthful responses to the questions that lead to your development and statement of these values, not those which you feel are "correct" or that you believe others would want you to embrace. When determining these values, it would be helpful to find a convenient time and place when you are alone and completely relaxed. Meditation is a powerful resource for this exercise. Try to avoid interruptions, clocks, and telephones by creating a relaxed, conducive environment that will help pull "your truth" from your consciousness. This truth should speak to you and be based on your deep intuition. Don't expect immediate answers to your quest. In good time you will find that you will "move into the answers." It may take a day, a week, or a month. The answers will come. I promise you that; and when they do, you will experience a deep sense of peace and a passion to proceed. A brief summary of a relaxation technique that can help you achieve a meditative state is presented in Appendix B.

Reaching Your Goals in Each of the Spheres

Next, for each of these unifying principles and values, I have found it helpful to set a series of goals for the next one, three, and five years, with a more detailed focus on the upcoming year. Each goal should be accompanied by an action plan with specific dates. As an example, I share one goal from my Professional Sphere that I prepared for the year 2005. The complete plan for that year is provided in Appendix A. It was one of three goals I had in this sphere. Each of the spheres had one to three goals.

> ***One Goal in the Professional Sphere:*** Within three years, I will help build Chateau Mcely into an international successful retreat and spa, and within a five-year time frame I will create a program to bring leading thinkers and experts to the Czech Republic and to Chateau Mcely to discuss implementable solutions to challenging social issues such as energy security, climate change, and the need for more conscious leadership in business.

> *Actions to take to achieve this goal:*

> ❖ Complete reconstruction of Chateau Mcely and open for business by September 30.

❖ Recruit and train an effective core management team by March 1, 2005; lead team building and training exercises monthly—from March through December.

❖ Create an international marketing strategy by April 30, 2005.

❖ By April 30, 2005, establish a reliable mechanism to financially manage Chateau Mcely.

❖ Explore three to four mechanisms to create and brand a seminar program on Conscious or Inspired Leadership at Chateau Mcely by December 31, 2005.

❖ By December 31, 2007, establish a realistic budget and strategy for Chateau Mcely that projects a profit in 2008.

❖ Establish business opening. Soft opening: May 1, 2006; formal opening: September 1, 2006.

❖ Launch our website for Chateau Mcely by April 30.

❖ Complete a business plan for our Leadership Training Concept by April 15.

❖ Support the World Business Academy for up to five hours per week.

I suggest that you use this same process for your professional goals and also for each of the goals associated with your Financial, Relationship, Spirituality, Health, and Knowledge Spheres.

Finally, after this exercise is completed, to help maintain your life in balance, I found over the years that it is important to make the following commitment concerning time management.

Time Management Supports Life Balance

I balance my life within the Six Spheres for Personal and Professional Growth. I do so by reviewing daily how I spend my time and I adjust my actions, when necessary, to be in accord with proper and realistic balance of my values, goals, and actions.

I also have found it helpful to carry in my wallet or briefcase an abbreviated version of my one-year goals so that I can easily look at them each evening. The time management aspect of this process is so important because as any successful person who has achieved personal fulfillment will likely agree, *balance* in life is perhaps the most difficult part of this undertaking and generally requires constant attention to stay in accord with personal values.

Once this process is completed, it is only necessary to update your plan each year. Your values are unlikely to change, but your goals will change. This seems like a lot of work. It is. But it's worth the effort if you use the plan and maintain a balanced life to achieve the goals you set for yourself. The personal details in my plan are not important for you. What I offer you is its form and comprehensiveness, which hopefully can serve as a template to help you design your own personal plan that will support achieving your destiny.

It may seem like a lot of material, but once you are actively in the flow of implementing the actions specified, you will be surprised at how relatively straightforward the undertaking is and, more importantly, how very effective it is in progressing to your personal goals. The success of this method is based on a fundamental principle that I discovered many years ago: *you create your goals first in your mind, then on paper, and then you are able to perceive and manifest them as your reality.* The connecting field that governs this process is your personal consciousness. It has the potential of great and far-reaching power.[39] This, of course, has been known and practiced by Eastern philosophers for several millennia.

As I have argued, *success is achieving, in a timely manner, worthwhile goals that you set for yourself.* You will be amazed at what you can accomplish in a year, in a decade—in a lifetime.

CHAPTER 4

Lasting Happiness

Happiness is not a goal; it is a byproduct.[40]

—ELEANOR ROOSEVELT

KEY CONCEPTS

◆ Lasting happiness is always a byproduct and is never achieved as a direct goal.

◆ Although genetic predisposition has much to do with your innate happiness "set point," the larger contribution comes from a combination of your environment and what you do with your life, both of which are well within your control.

◆ Happiness results from following your true sense of *purpose* in all that you do.

◆ Your sense of *purpose* must draw on your personal *essence*—that special attribute that distinguishes you from others.

◆ *Purpose* leads to *passion* which ignites high levels of physical and emotional *energy* and unfolds *creativity*. This enables you to solve challenging problems, which generates *innovation*. The result is a *return* which may be financial, emotional, psychological, spiritual, or some combination of these. The final outcome is deep personal *gratitude*, the source of lasting happiness. The path described by this "Fulfillment Formula" is one of the most effective means to a lasting happiness.

EVERY YEAR THERE ARE LITERALLY HUNDREDS OF BOOKS and articles published on how to be happy, usually how to get *there* faster, or how to get more of *it*, however you wish to define "there" and "it." This is not a fad; it goes back thousands of years. Aristotle concluded some 2,300 years ago that more than anything else in life, people seek happiness, usually through beauty, money, or power, and this approach in and of itself never succeeds. Why? For one thing, happiness cannot be achieved directly as a goal; it is always the result of our doing something; as Eleanor Roosevelt rightfully noted, it's a byproduct.

What Is Happiness?

How does happiness truly unfold? What makes us happy? First, it helps to agree as to what we mean by "happiness." Most dictionaries define happiness as a state of mind characterized by feelings of contentment, love, satisfaction, pleasure, or joy, that is, personal fulfillment. I think we must also recognize that there is no such thing as constant happiness—except perhaps for a few "enlightened" saints who spend their lives in meditative bliss. But that's not the path for most of us. Our lives are generally lived somewhere between the poles of joy and sorrow, laughter and sighs, achievement and disappointment. The key is how to live a happy life on average. At the end of the day, a week, a month, a year—when you look back, do you feel that deep sense of fulfillment sought by the spirit inside you?

So, what leads to happiness? I think we must certainly live by our basic values, those personal rules and guidelines ingrained in our consciousness that set the arrow of the compass by which we journey through life. Those values may well vary from person to person. However, whatever they are, when we violate any of them we feel stressed, unsatisfied, and **unhappy**. But following your basic values is not enough to achieve lasting happiness and contentment. As the mathematicians would say, "It is a necessary but not sufficient condition."

The Happiness Formula

The pioneers of the Positive Psychology movement founded in the early 1990s struggled with the importance of genetics and environmental factors for our state of happiness. Are we born with a certain level of happiness or unhappiness? Is there anything we can control to lead us to a happier life? As biologists uncovered the details of the human genome, a more complete understanding of the contributions of nurture and nature began to unfold.[41]

It appears that genes have a significant impact on the range of our natural "set point" for happiness. If you have happy parents, it's quite possible that you too will have a predisposition for a high happiness set point; and of course the converse is true, as well. However, modern science has shown that genes are often sensitive to environmental conditions. Furthermore, you can have a significant impact on your state of happiness by addressing the conditions of your life and by what you do with it.

All of this has been somewhat "quantified" in the following qualitative equation developed by Martin Seligman and others who founded the Positive Psychology movement.[42]

$$H = S + C + V$$

Here, **H** is the level of *happiness* that you actually experience; **S** is your genetic *set* point; **C** is the environmental *conditions* of your life; and **V** is *voluntary* activities: what you do with your life. So, the challenge then, since **S** is fixed, is to see what you can do to increase **C** and **V**. Although the relative contributions of **S, C,** and **V** to happiness can be argued, most psychologists would say that for a normal healthy person the relative contributing weights are approximately: **S** = 40%; **C** = 20%; and **V** = 40%. Therefore, beyond choosing the "right" parents, your primary impact potential is on **C** and **V**, and it can be quite significant, about 60 percent.

As for **C**, there are several factors that have been found to contribute and which, if addressed can have a positive impact.[43] The first is *noise level.* Research has shown that people who have to adapt continuously to high levels of noise find it difficult to do so and this has a diminishing effect on their level of happiness. The old adage that people living close to an airport or a train station adapt to the noise level is not correct. They basically learn to tolerate the noise with varying levels of subconscious stress. It's difficult to be happy when you're stressed and annoyed, even when this distress is subconscious.[44]

In this modern, connected world, *long-distance commuting* also has a negative impact on happiness. I recall when living in the New York City area that it was not uncommon for some people who lived on Long Island to travel to work two hours each way in heavy traffic. Research shows that those who do travel extended distances to work exhibit significant stress levels on the job and a diminished state of happiness.[45]

A lack of control decreases the level of happiness. Haidt and Rodin have demonstrated that changing an institution's environment to increase a sense of personal control among its occupants, such as patients in a hospital, students in school, or workers on the assembly line, was one of the most effective means to increase their sense of engagement, energy, and happiness.[46] For example, in a most remarkable study by Langer and Rodin, two floors of patients in a nursing home were studied. On one floor patients were allowed to choose flowers and plants for their room, care for the plants, and choose a specific movie night each week as well as the movie to view. On a separate floor the nurses chose the plants, watered them, and chose the movie night and the movie.

This seemingly minor manipulation had significant effects. On the floor where patients had increased control, they were happier, more active, and more alert, as rated by both the doctors and nurses, and these benefits were still observed even after eighteen months. Furthermore, during the subsequent eighteen months the floor patients with greater control amazingly had statistically significantly better health and half as many deaths—15 percent versus 30 percent.[47] Isn't it amazing what a small increase in the level of personal autonomy can do to increase self-esteem, happiness, and health? Think what this can do for employees. What an opportunity!

Shame is another controllable factor that impacts your level of environmental happiness. People who remove any physical or intellectual trait that is responsible for their feeling self-conscious generally increase their level of happiness. A large percentage of plastic surgery is directed at these kinds of "patients,"[48] often with very positive outcomes.

And finally, and surely not surprisingly, one of the major factors that is controllable in the **C** factor of the happiness equation is *relationships*. This factor is sometimes thought to trump all other components of **C** in the equation. As may be expected, good relationships make people happy, and happy people enjoy more and better relationships than unhappy people.[49]

An important subset of the relationship factor is the loss of a close and satisfying relationship. Two recent studies show that living alone or suffering loneliness as a consequence of loss of a spouse or significant other can not only lead to intense unhappiness, but also raises the person's risk of dying from heart disease or, for that matter, from any other cause.[50] As Three Dog Night proclaimed in their 1969 hit song, "One is the loneliest number that you'll ever do." It can also be the unhappiest and deadliest number.

Once **S** is fixed by the genetic code and **C** is addressed as best it can be, this leaves only **V**, the most significant factor after **S** to control your level of happiness. If you are in balance with respect to your basic values, I have found that the fundamental remaining requirement for optimal happiness is that you continuously pursue your sense of purpose, your raison d'être, as the French would say. And this means applying your personal essence to create value for both the world and for you.

As Aristotle found during his studies more than three thousand years ago, this seems to be one of humanity's best kept secrets. Many of us seek happiness exclusively through money, power, sex, or some combination of the three. However, as discussed in chapter 2, each of us is born with a personal essence, that fundamental capability or skill that differentiates us from others in our social and professional circles. *And when we find that special piece of us and apply it in whatever we do, especially to a positive need in the world, it generates personal passion and high levels of emotional and physical energy—an incredible force that evaporates fear, unleashes creativity, and has been known to change the world.* That's the true formula for long-term happiness. It works every time!

Personal Purpose and Passion

Paulo Coelho, author of *The Alchemist,* tells us in this wonderful and incisive fable that all of us know what our personal essence is when we are quite young. But the ways of the world have the effect of dulling our senses. By the time we are adults, we often either forget what that special asset is, or we have been talked out of it by others. We don't think in these terms when we are youngsters, but that special skill is there, and it can be kindled or rekindled in the strangest and most unexpected way.

As I relayed in the telling of my life story, I have had a life-long passion for and involvement in the businesses of technology and entertainment. I maintain that my personal predilection for science and technology was always there; I was born with it. The chemistry set I received when I was eight years old simply ignited an innate spark into a flame and as a consequence my skill and interest became obvious not only to me, but to those around me, as well.

Similarly, my desire as a youngster to find an "inside job" drew on my innate natural magnetic attraction to rock and roll music and to perform as an entertainer. Even my passion for writing, my mother tells me, was exposed by a gift of a children's typewriter which my parents gave me for my ninth birthday. Now at ninety-one years of age, she still recalls me sitting for hours at that slow machine writing tales of science fiction. For the longest time in my early youth, she kept one of my essays entitled "Trip to Titan," which I am sure was the result of my interest in both writing and science.

As I pursued my journey in both entertainment and science in parallel, and as tiresome and challenging as it often was doing both, I found myself frequently saying, "This is fantastic; it's a blast!" I was deeply grateful for the opportunity. I believe that "grateful" is the key word here. Why? Because I have seen this kind of passion-based journey played out by other people who are content and experience long-term happiness.

A simple but profound human equation that should be remembered is what I call the "Fulfillment Formula." Following your sense of **Purpose** based on your innate *Essence* when connected to a *Need* that makes this a better world, leads to *Passion*, which ignites high levels of physical and emotional *Energy*. This unleashes *Creativity* that generates *Innovation* to provide you with a *Return*—financial, emotional, psychological, spiritual, or some combination of the four. This ultimately endows us with a deep sense of *Gratitude*, the source of all lasting *Happiness*.

Essence → Purpose → Need → Passion → Energy →
Creativity → Innovation → Return →
Gratitude → HAPPINESS

It's not beauty, power, or money. It's not that these factors are unimportant, but as Jigmi Thinley, the Prime Minister of Bhutan exclaimed so eloquently in his 2010 address before the United Nations General Assembly, "Happiness comes from a judicious equilibrium between gains in material comfort and growth of the mind and spirit in a just and sustainable environment."[51] Bhutan is world famous for its commitment since 1972 to the concept of Gross National Happiness (GNH) as opposed to the classical Gross Domestic Product (GDP). Although challenging to quantify mathematically, there have been extensive studies to do so.[52] The Bhutanese use the concept in the five-year plan for their nation, and follow their strategies with discipline. They tend to be a happy and content nation!

It is my firm belief that only when there is a significant global shift in consciousness to respect, quantify, and foster the value of human happiness and fulfillment, will we muster the courage and commitment to use existing technologies and know-how to create a just, peaceful, and sustainable future for all.

I think we are at a critical time in human history, close to a precarious tipping point. We can either fall further into the abyss that currently is being created by the challenges that face our global community, or we can transition to a new exciting and productive paradigm. This new way of "being" is espoused and highlighted by an increasing number of change-makers throughout the world, thinkers at higher levels of consciousness, who recognize what is at stake and seek to help create a world where everyone has the opportunity to be happy.

Happiness in the Workplace

For those of us in business, it behooves us to place our employees in jobs and an environment that is most effective in tapping into their personal essence and sense of purpose in this world. This is a challenging undertaking but the rewards for both employees and company are significant. We saw in chapter 2 that an extensive global study reported by corporate strategist guru Gary Hamel showed that only 20 percent of people are happy in their jobs.[53] Why is that? A lack of purpose causes anxiety and people then tend to work inefficiently. Modern business consultants like to say they are not "engaged" in their work. Can you imagine the level of productivity and collective sense of fulfillment and happiness if we were to tap into only a fraction of our employee's personal essence and sense of purpose? This might well provide the ultimate competitive advantage!

So then, what instills and reinforces a sense of personal purpose, thereby leading to happiness in the workplace? I believe this occurs when the following key elements are addressed:

The challenges in a job must draw on the person's personal essence.

It does no good to ask a plumber to do an electrician's job. If you are an employer, it is of paramount importance that you do your best to hire the *right* person for the *right* job at the *right* time, and when you make a mistake that you exit that person with grace, dignity, and compassion as soon as possible. It is in both the company's and the employee's best interest to do so. As we shall see in Part III, this is a very difficult task, but it is one of the most important factors in building a successful company.

Furthermore, it is important to work with employees to uncover the nature of their assets and strengths. The investment in time and money is more than worth the effort. At Chateau Mcely we do this by multiple recruitment interviews and day-long assessment tests conducted by skilled human resource practitioners. This is followed by periodic discussions with our employees throughout the year, as well as personal coaching and training, when indicated as beneficial.

Even after all of this effort, we still make mistakes, but overall it has led to a happier, committed team. If you would like some guidance concerning your fundamental innate strengths and capabilities, consider taking the strengths test developed by Martin Seligman, one of the founders of Positive

Psychology. It can be accessed free of charge at his website.[54] Similar products can be found at Lance Secretan's website.[55]

The job or position must appeal to the employee's need to "help the greater good."

As I previously stated, this may be one of the world's best kept secrets—whether they know it or not, almost everyone wants to do something meaningful, to make a positive difference in this world. It is up to the employer to find the means to articulate a vision and mission that captures the excitement and imagination of employees; it is best to keep it simple and state it in one sentence as the company's *Dream* so that all employees can remember and embrace it.

It doesn't matter whether it is an insurance company or a hospital, management must articulate an inspiring vision as to how their company is helping to make this a better world. At Catalytica Pharmaceuticals our corporate dream was to *"Produce the lowest cost pharmaceuticals using the cleanest technology."* Our nearly 2,000 employees found it easy and motivational to embrace this dream. Most of us had family and friends who were finding it increasingly challenging to pay the rapidly rising prices at the pharmacy. We felt a deep sense of passion because we were part of making this a better world.

At a recent business breakfast meeting, I met an executive and inquired as to what business he was in. He replied that he was in the business of manufacturing, marketing, and selling beer. Perhaps a more inspirational way of answering my question might have been something like, "Our company is in the business of stimulating relaxation, conversation, and fostering friendship and hospitality by providing people with the best beer in the world!"

There should be a reasonable probability of success in achieving any goals that are set.

No one wants to work hard without some level of accomplishment. One way to keep employees motivated when there are a number of challenging and longer-term goals to achieve, is to be sure that there are some short-term easier goals that demonstrate progress toward the final endpoint. This is particularly an issue for employees working in research and development. Drawing on a baseball metaphor, this is what I call a "singles" strategy. You can't focus only on all "home runs;" you need to hit some "singles" along the way to demonstrate progress toward the final goal and thereby maintain the employee's motivation and focus.

Employees should be provided with a fair level of autonomy.

It's best to hire good people, work with them to develop a set of specific goals that support the company objectives, and then let them decide how best to get the work done. Recall my discussion of the study by Langer and Rodin, where they observed a significant increase in self-esteem, happiness, and health when patients were given even modest increased levels of control in their lives.[56] We all like to have a reasonable level of autonomy over what we do. This is what motivates us, and when we are thus motivated we often find creative solutions that would not otherwise be obvious.

Employees should share in any success that they help achieve.

This could include public and private positive feedback, bonuses, a salary raise, stock options, and as we do at Chateau Mcely, meaningful profit sharing at the end of the year. Notice that monetary rewards are in last place. After a reasonable level of financial stability, money is not the primary driving force for most people.

Some Final Thoughts about Happiness

I think that Jonathan Haidt does a fine job in summarizing the nature of happiness in his book *The Happiness Hypothesis*:[57]

> Happiness is not something that you can find or acquire, or achieve directly. You have to get the conditions right and then wait. Some of those conditions are within you, such as coherence among the parts and levels of your personality. Other conditions require relationships to things beyond you: Just as plants need sun, water, and a good soil to thrive, people need love, work, and a connection to something larger. It is worth striving to get the right relationships between yourself and others, between yourself and work, and between yourself and something larger than yourself. If you get these relationships right a sense of purpose and meaning will emerge.

Whenever I speak with young people who are trying to determine how to plan their professional life, I usually offer them the following ideas to consider:

People usually approach the work they do for the following reasons:

A Job—to make money.

A Career—to achieve professional goals of advancement, promotion, and prestige.

A Calling—work that is intrinsically fulfilling because it builds on your personal essence, creates your passion, and contributes to the greater good.

Although a Career is a fine endeavor, a Calling is by far the best means to deep, long-term, lasting happiness and personal fulfillment. And it more often than not results in significant returns.

Don't plan to be wealthy as your personal goal in life. When you do good by producing high-quality work for the greater good, you very often do well and achieve wealth, prestige, and advancement.

There are numerous examples: Steve Jobs–Apple; Bill Gates–Microsoft; Sergey Brin and Larry Page–Google; Anita Roddick–The Body Shop and many more less well-known successful individuals. None of them set out to be wealthy. They were passionate about what they were doing and relished the journey.

Don't waste your time trying to live someone else's life.

Early on in life, generally as a youngster, you likely discovered what drives you, what your purpose is. It is important to follow that little voice inside. Hopefully, you have people around you who support your ambitions but if not and you lose sight of your purpose in life, even as a mature adult, you can recapture it. I promise you that!

Don't be trapped by dogma, living blindly with other people's thinking.[58]

Yes, listen to understand the views of others and integrate their thinking into your own as you see fit. Be sure it feels right, and if not, don't do it. Rarely does someone else's "It can't be done!" turn out to be correct. Running the mile in less than four minutes was once thought by many athletic trainers to be biomechanically impossible for a human being, until Roger Bannister broke that record on May 6, 1954. Subsequently, within one year, several other runners broke the record as well, after "They knew it could be done!"

Don't let the opinion of others drown out your inner voice.[59]

That little computer inside you is quite powerful and integrates lots of variables, both consciously and unconsciously. Don't sell it short! When you have dwelled on a point in meditative quiet for some time and you hear clearly that little voice from within telling you what to do, you have moved into the answer. Trust your consciousness and follow its directive.

Happiness is often thought to be elusive and challenging to find. Actually, it's within your reach. All you need to do is be yourself. Embrace your essence, whatever it may be. It's the true you and something to be treasured. In using that essence to do good in the world, you will also do well personally and succeed. You will find lasting happiness.

CHAPTER 5

The Power of Passion, the Failure of Fear

Passion is the first step to achievement. Passion increases your willpower. Passion changes you. Passion makes the impossible possible.[60]

—JOHN C. MAXWELL

KEY CONCEPTS

◈ The emotional stress and fear induced by upheavals in the economy and by rapid technological and social change often cause people to ignore critical global challenges, especially if there is a shred of opposing evidence of their future significance.

◈ Major positive change, whether in individuals or in organizations, only occurs through the inspiring effects of pure passion.

◈ Passion happens naturally when four elements fall seamlessly into place:

We tap into our innate talents—our very **essence**—applying them in areas of personal interest and capability.

We work for the greater good.

We see periodic progress towards the ultimate goal.

We perceive a genuine promise of appropriate reward for success.

ALTHOUGH MANY PEOPLE ARE AWARE of the devastating consequences of critical global issues such as non-transparent economic inequities, oil depletion, climate change, nuclear proliferation, and poverty, why is it that we appear to do almost nothing as the clock ticks forward? Many of us are paralyzed in disbelief or denial, as though there will be no ill effects in our lifetime, if ever. Why? I believe there are several potent reasons for this.

Financial Motives Create Inaction

Consider the problem of global oil depletion as viewed on the North American continent and in Europe and its impact on energy security and climate change. There are strong financial reasons not to jar the status quo. Corporations have invested billions of dollars in plants and infrastructure to support the current energy use. To them, change would come at an unacceptable financial investment. Politicians don't want to lose support from these major corporate sponsors. For example, because of financial support from oil companies some politicians are reluctant to champion non-fossil fuel, carbon-free technologies regardless of their potential to mitigate the challenges of energy security and climate change. Although end-of-year data are not yet available, in 2012, to maintain their good standing with the global fossil fuel industry, it was estimated that politicians would provide that industry with financial subsidies in excess of $775 billion, possibly reaching $1 trillion for the year.[61]

This is a short-sighted perspective, but it often brings these politicians handsome short-term financial returns. Until recently and only subsequent to immense shareholder pressure, did ExxonMobil change its negative posture concerning the science behind global climate change and the realities of oil depletion. In fact, it is well documented that the company has handsomely supported a minority of scientists and consultant groups who claim that climate change and oil depletion are a nonissue.

A Major Challenge—Lifestyle Changes for the Common Good

It has often been stated that if the possible solutions to our problems require a level of personal sacrifice or cutting back on our comfortable lifestyles, we resist such change. Most of us don't easily give up our creature comforts, especially after having them for so long at low cost. It's like taking a child into a sweet shop, buying her an ice cream and then asking her to give it up. Thus Americans have received low-taxed, cheap oil for so long that they don't easily give up their gas-guzzling Sport Utility Vehicles (SUV). Although declining in numbers due to higher oil prices, in 2008 nearly 50 percent of the 250 million registered vehicles in the United States were SUVs. Fortunately, the consequences of increasing energy prices are forcing auto companies to admit to a more realistic picture. Once-powerful, global enterprises such as Chrysler and GM, which heavily marketed these inefficient vehicles to the American public, may very well be on their way to becoming distant memories unless they change dramatically.

Anxiety and Fear Breed Rationalization

But there is a much more fundamental reason, the most powerful effect of all. I call it the Law of Human Survival: *human beings under the emotional and economic stress of rapid technological and social change ignore immense global challenges if it is convenient and "reasonably rational" to perceive that they will occur in the distant future, and particularly if there is even a shred of opposing evidence that these challenges may not be nearly as significant as thought.* This is our great escape clause. We join in the support of industries that are fighting change, "We need more data, more evidence, just to be sure!" Then we put the issue on the shelf and out of our mind.

The "shred of opposing evidence" effect is the basis for a powerful public relations strategy and was used very effectively and successfully for decades by tobacco companies to cast doubt on the ill-health effects of cigarettes. "Lung cancer and cardiovascular disease, we doubt it! We need more data!" Many of the same public relations firms who perfected this strategy now work for some fossil fuel companies dismissing or substantially diminishing the realities of global climate change and oil depletion.

There is only so much stress-induced fear we can handle. Fear constricts the human psyche. It creates a vortex of emotional pain from which we must escape. Sure, fear has its place. In the battlefield, "Keep your head down, or it will be shot off," works quite well. But not when it comes to developing creative solutions to challenging problems. There are few great innovations in this world that have been created out of motivation by fear.

Evolutionary theory and records seem to indicate that as for most species, human beings do best when they cooperate with each other. However, world renowned Harvard biologist E. O. Wilson thinks that maybe human beings are hardwired not to worry about future generations. He points out that, "For hundreds of millennia, those who worked for the short-term gain within a small circle of relatives and friends lived longer and left more offspring—even when their collective striving caused their children and empires to crumble around them. The long view that might have saved their distant descendants required a vision and extended altruism instinctively difficult to marshal."[62]

I hope and tend to believe that over the past several generations human consciousness has evolved some distance beyond this hardwired, self-centered protection mechanism and thus we can achieve a productive and sustainable future. There is only so much fear we can take, and currently there is more than enough to go around without having to overwhelm our spirit with a heavy dose of future fears. Yet, for challenges such as poverty, energy security, nuclear proliferation, and global climate change, we must act now if there is to be a positive outcome which minimizes the negative impact on humanity and creates a promising future for our children.

Overcoming Our Protracted Paralysis

In my opinion, there is only one force that can erase this self-protecting, laissez-faire attitude towards critical global challenges, or any critical change for that matter. **It is the energy of unbridled passion.** This creative force is so powerful that it evaporates fear from the deepest level of the human spirit and can literally change the world. It has done this so many times before. Think back in your own life to when you achieved a significant accomplishment; perhaps a sports medal, or a college degree, or an award for some achievement; or perhaps it was reaching a goal you set for yourself concerning fitness or academic excellence. Almost certainly this required an intense level of passion, and the more difficult the challenge, the more passion it required, ultimately yielding a deep sense of fulfillment.

Most often a passionate vision starts within a single person. Recall Leonardo da Vinci, Rachel Carson, Isaac Newton, Marie Curie, Thomas Edison, Maria Montessori, Albert Einstein, Jonas Salk, Margaret Thatcher, and thousands of lesser known change-makers who left their indelible imprint on our planet. Each of them discovered their personal capability or essence and connected it with an important need in the world. In doing so they became driven by a personal vision that ignited their passion, and that "spark" ultimately became a "flame," which in turn became a "torch," and it changed the world.[63] Unbridled passion is like that. No barrier is too high.

It is arguably the most significant competitive advantage an individual or a company can have. It has been estimated that most people work at less than 30 percent of their full efficiency. World-renowned corporate strategy expert, Gary Hamel, has shown that a mere 21 percent of employees are engaged in their work.[64] Nearly 80 percent could care less about their job. And of the 80 percent, nearly four out of ten people, that is, 32 percent of the total, are mostly or entirely disengaged.

In my opinion, this is due to the fear and anxiety that accompanies a lack of purpose. They are "unmotivated," simply going through the motions.

Although motivation is always self-generated, passion can be fostered by creating an environment that addresses a person's need for greater purpose. Every one of us is born with this need. This can result in human efficiencies beyond 90 percent. Did you ever do something so motivating that you lost track of time and your desire for food, water, or sleep?

The study referred to by Hamel demonstrates that most managers have failed to grasp the direct correlation between profitability and what I like to call "Employment Enjoyment." As he points out, "Lasting success depends on a company's ability to unleash the initiative, imagination and passion of its employees at all levels, and this can only happen if all of those folks are connected heart and soul with their work, their company and its mission. They see and feel the dream."

Take the example of the Apple iPhone. Apple's development team was led personally by Apple's deceased cofounder and CEO Steve Jobs. I had a number of conversations with Steve over the years as he was my neighbor in Palo Alto, California. His management style is highly controversial. I believe the same results are achievable using a more positive form of Inspired Leadership, and in doing so, the achievements can be longer lasting without the personnel damage created by his style of management. This aspect is discussed in further detail in chapter 7.

Jobs was a bipolar leader. Things were either "insanely great" or pure "trash," to use a more acceptable word than his usual descriptor. However, he did get incredible results. He hired the very best people, people who wanted to change the world, and when they made a mistake, he often fired them immediately. Jobs' passion for detail and perfection is legendary, and this spirit permeated the talented team members he hired and those he kept as his "A-Team" players.

As a consequence, Apple was able to jump into the mobile phone market quickly and with absolutely no industry experience. The first iPhone was released in June 2007. In the third quarter of 2009 the iPhone division delivered $1.6 billion in profits, while Nokia, the world's largest mobile phone producer, earned just $1.1 billion in profits. What makes these figures so amazing is that at the time Nokia had 35 percent of the global market while Apple's share was less than 3 percent.

The lesson here is that you don't have to be the biggest to be the most profitable, but you do have to be the most highly differentiated—all those wonderful iPhone features and "apps"—and that differentiation is driven by "Employment Enjoyment," i.e., proactive, inventive, zealous, employees—

people with **Passion**.[65] While Jobs could be super intense, unforgiving and often verbally whipped his team when their performance did not meet his expectations, within but a nanosecond he could return to the other pole and build up their egos with such finesse and spirit that they often performed "miracles" they thought not to be possible. However, in the end, this schizophrenic approach broke many human spirits. As I found from my experience, and as I profess throughout this book, Inspired Leadership is much more powerful, much longer lasting, and much more personally rewarding for all concerned.

You cannot order people to be enthusiastic, creative, and passionate. But if the elements are right, passion in employees can make a huge difference. They can help change the world for the better.

So how do we create an environment that instills such passion? I think there are five components that must be present:

1. APPLYING THE POWER OF EACH PERSON'S ESSENCE

The goal or objective must take advantage of an individual's innate strengths and capabilities, his or her essence, and apply them in an area of their personal interest.

I have a friend, George, a talented electrician who as a young boy loved to tinker with ham radio kits, electric clocks, and stereo sets. By the time he was in his early teens, George had learned to fix just about any household electrical device—toasters, radios, televisions—you name it. He won prizes in several local science projects and went on to start and build a successful electrical service company. On the other hand, George dislikes plumbing problems— he always has—and would be loath to take one on. When he has a plumbing problem at his home, he calls a plumber.

2. ENCOURAGING THE DESIRE TO WORK FOR THE GREATER GOOD

The challenge must appeal to a person's need to help humanity.

This is the key ingredient of unbridled passion. Both Gandhi and Edison, two disparate innovators, thought that their pursuits would change the world for the better. They never had any doubt. Unless people see that mega-issues such as global climate change and energy security are going to significantly affect them immediately, they are unlikely to do much about these problems unless their perception and perspective are altered by creating a personal penchant and passion for positive action that will make this a better world to live in.

This kind of change only occurs by stimulating and exciting the human spirit. *People must perceive and believe deep down in their bones that they are part of a team that will change the world for the better.* That's the magic. It has been done before quite successfully. The Apple iPhone Team had no doubt that their "insanely great" mobile phone would change the world of telephony. As Steve Jobs put it, "We want to put a dent in the universe."

U.S. President John F. Kennedy galvanized Americans after the successful launch of the Soviet Union's Sputnik satellite. He raised America's passion by his personal commitment to what some saw as a daunting goal, "We must and we will put a man on the moon in less than one decade." And we did. Not surprisingly, the Greek philosopher, Epictetus once commented: "*Not by facts, but by perceptions is society governed.*"

Kennedy inspired and led the achievement of this goal, but not by stimulating our fear of the communist Soviet Union. He ignited America's excitement to demonstrate its scientific prowess and show its technological leadership by forging a key step in our understanding and exploration of space and the universe. NASA was formed, which not only achieved this goal, but also spawned numerous new technologies and companies to ultimately create millions of jobs globally and stimulate the world economy with trillions of dollars of GDP. Millions of Americans participated in the space program financially, physically, and spiritually. When you do good for the "whole," you do amazingly well for all, much beyond your greatest expectations. NASA is a good example.

The largest TV audience in history watched in awe as every space shot was televised around the globe. And on that momentous day, July 20, 1969, when Apollo 11 landed on the moon and Neil Armstrong became the first human being to set foot on its surface, billions of people around the planet joined us to share in that event. In some ways, at that very moment we were ONE. Armstrong recognized this "oneness" and universal sharing for the greater good with his first words upon setting foot on the moon's surface: "That's one small step for a man; one giant step for mankind."[66]

This was an all out "space race" between the United States and the Soviet Union, and as any good runner will tell you, a race is won by a passion to do your absolute personal best and never by the fear of failure. More often than not, your fear will deliver what you are afraid of.

3. DEMONSTRATION OF A VIABLE STRATEGY

Even though the big picture might entail a long-term plan of magnificent magnitude toward admirable goals, there must be a perceived and reasonable probability of a few near-term small successes on the way to the bigger goal.

Most people have a difficult time working on challenging long-term goals with limited or no positive feedback along the way. As I mentioned earlier, drawing on an American baseball analogy, don't try for all "home runs." Hit a few singles, they come sooner. People need positive feedback; it's a powerful motivator. They need to know they are on the right track. This does a number of valuable things. With companies, it motivates employees, it demonstrates the validity and viability of the corporate strategy, and it increases the value of the company in the eyes of current and potential shareholders.

Some years ago, when I was Chairman of Catalytica, Inc., we had a strategy that for several years was focused on hitting only "home runs." This strategy was in many ways a consequence of our venture financing. Venture capitalists tend to look for projects that will both change the world and can be achieved in a relatively short time frame. For example, with PetroCanada and Mitsubishi Oil, we were developing a process that if successful would, in a single-process step, inexpensively convert natural gas to a liquid fuel that could be easily shipped safely anywhere in the world. This technology would do away with the need for expensive liquefied natural gas (LNG) transport, which requires special costly high-pressure, refrigerated tankers, and is considered a dangerous technology and a security risk. We were also working with several large energy companies on catalytic combustion technology as a means to burn fuels with no or minimal resultant pollution. Both of these goals had previously been the target of billions of dollars of research by several multinational companies around the globe. All of their efforts had been unsuccessful.

These were very challenging technologies—"home runs"—and we spent millions of dollars in their development. Our stock price languished along the way as investors wondered whether we would ever solve these problems and commercialize the technologies. Finally, we decided to hit a "few singles" to demonstrate the commercial viability of our technologies which involved the molecular engineering or design of efficient catalysts for the low-cost manufacture of desirable products with minimal formation of undesirable byproducts. We continued to work on a few of our long-term home runs, but we displaced some of our efforts in that area with a solid approach to demonstrating our practical commercial capabilities. We were determined to hit a couple of singles.

We identified pharmaceuticals as an industry where our knowledge in catalytic science could have a reasonably quick and positive impact by enabling us to manufacture drugs in a more ecologically friendly manner and at lower cost. Our strategy was straightforward. First, we would demonstrate that our technological know-how could be applied to produce some of the simple molecules used to manufacture the final active ingredients in existing drugs. Then we would acquire a small production plant to show that we could manufacture these building blocks cleanly, inexpensively, and with the regulatory-required *Good Manufacturing Practices*. Next, we would look for opportunities to integrate forward and produce the final active drug ingredients.

We quickly demonstrated our capabilities, which led to a $15 million investment by Pfizer Pharmaceuticals and ultimately the growth of Catalytica Pharmaceuticals, in less than five years, from essentially a few people to a public company valued at more than $1 billion. At one point our stock price tripled. Ultimately, we hit a technological home run in our other areas of research, but it was the singles along the way that helped us get there. And in fact, much to our surprise, our success in pharmaceuticals had escalated from a "single" to a "home run!"

4. SHARING THE RETURNS OF SUCCESS WITH ALL STAKEHOLDERS

There should be a perceived and actual benefit for all involved, whether it is financial, social, psychological, or some combination of all three.

You must share the wealth fairly in any successes, whatever that wealth may be. If it is the populace supporting a political agenda, such as a strategy to address energy security or climate change, then any tangible successes should bring near-term benefits to the populace, for instance, tax rebates and other financial incentives. If it's a company, employees should know from the start that they will be appropriately rewarded psychologically and financially with promotions and perhaps with stock options. The latter is particularly powerful as it provides employees with a sense of corporate ownership. When Catalytica was successful, even the janitors received a few shares of stock options. Ultimately Catalytica brought significant returns to **all** of its stakeholders, including employees, customers, investors, the community, and our suppliers. It was a win-win outcome all the way around.

5. ESTABLISHING A CLEAR VISION AND MISSION TO FORM A BETTER WORLD

Whether you seek to motivate employees or citizens of a nation toward a challenging goal, it is imperative that you create, articulate, and support a clear vision that stimulates in them a passion to participate in a journey that will make this a better world.

Anything short of that will significantly diminish your chances of success. Managers should assign employees to positions that take advantage of their innate strengths, capabilities, and predilections. Show them how they can make a difference for the greater good. Present a long-term strategy with visible, achievable, near-term successes—hit a few solid "singles." Let them play an active role in developing that part of the strategic plan which will impact them. This creates ownership and commitment. And be sure there s something in success for everyone.

The discovery of America, Marco Polo's voyage to China, and Thomas Edison's invention of the light bulb were based on passion, not fear. The latter rarely works to create something new and innovative. Fear has never changed the world for the better; but it certainly has done the converse. The Spanish Inquisition, the devastating impact of World Wars I and II, and the Holocaust are but a few examples of fear-induced courses of action.

All of this is particularly poignant at this point in history. As a species, we have not only evolved physically, but we have also evolved in the nebulous realm of consciousness. Many modern philosophers would argue that on average we have a much higher level of consciousness than our forerunners, the generations before us.[67] Creative, innovative people are generally at high levels of consciousness and do not work well in autocratic command and control operations. What we so desperately need now is a few courageous leaders stimulating people around the planet with the passion necessary to create a safe, rewarding, and sustainable future for all of our children. It can be done. Interested? Please step forward!

PART III

Building a Successful Business

Discover Inspired Leadership
Create an Innovative Environment
Share Success with All Stakeholders

CHAPTER 6

Building a Successful Company

*Individual commitment to a group effort—that is what
makes a team work, a company work, a society work,
a civilization work.*[68]

—VINCE LOMBARDI

KEY CONCEPTS

Eight actions taken together can lead to long-term success in *any*
business created and operated *anywhere*:

- Committing to the best practices of a skilled and inspired leader—charisma is not a requirement
- Hiring the right people at the right time for the right position, and immediately and compassionately arranging for those to leave who do not work out
- Coaching employees to develop corporate values to which they are committed
- Addressing a growing market, better yet, creating one
- Focusing strictly and passionately on the best opportunities
- Targeting an early commercial success, even a modest one
- Supporting all stakeholders—customers, employees, shareholders, suppliers, and community—so that they endorse the corporate dream
- Having a specific plan, embraced by all employees, but staying flexible

My Journey

In 1974, during the greatest recession in the United States subsequent to
World War II, I left a well-paying, secure position as Director of Catalyst
Research & Development at Exxon to cofound Catalytica Associates
Inc , a consulting firm focused in catalytic technologies. *Our specific technical skill was a deep and detailed scientific, engineering, and commercial
knowledge that enabled us to design commercially successful catalysts that
would facilitate industrial chemical processes to make only or primarily the*

desired product. This skill can have profound positive economic and ecological implications.

Catalysis is nanotechnology at its best with the desirable outcome of lower manufacturing costs and the elimination or minimization of environmental issues. In fact, catalysis was true nanotechnology much before that term became in vogue as a means to found and finance companies that create materials and products at the molecular level. For example, during the 1950s, Karl Ziegler of Germany and Giulio Natta of Italy created the famous molecular Ziegler-Natta catalysts based on titanium and aluminum. These catalysts were the prime force in creating a multibillion dollar polyolefin petrochemical industry, producing the products polyethylene and polypropylene. For this, Ziegler and Natta shared the 1963 Nobel Prize in chemistry. The importance of catalysis to science and society is further highlighted by the twenty Nobel Prizes in chemistry given so far over the years for scientific advances in catalysis.

Located in Silicon Valley, my business partners and I found ourselves surrounded by no shortage of brilliant, creative people and the appropriate infrastructure to support our entrepreneurial aspirations. Using these assets, over the next decade our team of talented people built a profitable enterprise of nearly one hundred employees with annual revenues of some $20 million. We helped many large companies: saving them time and money, minimizing their environmental issues, and simultaneously we became knowledgeable of critical problems and issues in emerging chemically-based businesses. By the early 1980s we were acknowledged as world experts in catalytic science and technologies.

With time, we recognized that while we saved our clients millions of dollars, we were paid strictly for our time at an hourly rate. We began to wonder if we were selling our knowledge and know-how too cheaply. Even more important, we questioned whether this was the best way for us to build a profitable business that would maximize its positive impact or the world. It certainly did not seem the best formula for growth. If we were to have received a percentage of our client's annual savings, it would have been a more acceptable arrangement. Unfortunately, in those days, due to corporate bureaucracies, it was nearly impossible to negotiate such a contract, especially as we had no idea when we signed an agreement just how significantly we would improve our client's product or process. We decided that it was time to take our next big strategic step—a transition into manufacturing based on our own proprietary technologies.

We created a strategy to develop and sharpen our skills in manufacturing and simultaneously leverage our technological expertise. As consultants, we found there were only so many hours in a day we could sell, and influencing the implementation of our ideas was limited. By developing our ideas, and in particular by entering manufacturing, we felt we could surely have a much greater positive impact on the world. Furthermore, we would have complete control on the quality of the results and the effectiveness in bringing our products and processes to the marketplace.

We focused on two growing markets that would benefit from our know-how and technologies—pharmaceuticals and sustainable energy generation. Two business units were formed—Catalytica Energy Systems, Inc. (CESI) and Catalytica Pharmaceuticals, Inc. (CPI).[69] CESI developed catalytic systems that enable the production of low-cost, clean energy and power. It focused on diesel engines, gas-fired turbines for electric power generation, and biomass-derived electric power.

In CPI we developed low-cost, environmentally-friendly processes to manufacture drugs for major pharmaceutical companies. Our goal was not only to help create a cleaner environment, but also to provide lower cost drugs to an aging population, which was finding it increasingly challenging to pay for costly prescriptions. Most of us had family members or friends who were deeply stressed by this healthcare issue. Our vision motivated all of our employees as it was truly a means to do "well" by doing "good;" however, I can assure you that we were much more passionate about doing "good" than doing "well."

To launch this strategy and grow our company we raised nearly $250 million through venture capital and public financial offerings. Catalytica became one of Silicon Valley's fastest growing companies. Within five years, CPI progressed from several people and no sales to about 1,800 people, nearly $500 million in revenues, and $50 million in profit. We acquired three pharmaceutical plants and raised our market value to approximately $1 billion. CPI manufactured over fifty drugs for international companies such as GlaxoSmithKline, e.g., Zidovudine® (AZT) for treating AIDS, Zovirax® (acyclovir) for treating viral infections, Wellbutrin® for depression. Lanoxin® (digitalis) for heart disease, and Zyban® (bupropion) for smoking cessation. In 2000 the pharmaceutical arm of DSM, the large corporate giant in the Netherlands made our shareholders "an offer they couldn't refuse." We sold CPI for over $800 million and made many shareholders very happy.

The Right Way to Achieve Success

We made some mistakes in building Catalytica; fortunately none was significant enough to have a lasting impact. More importantly, we learned one way—certainly not the only way—to create a successful business. Looking back, it is simple to summarize our prescription for success but it was quite challenging to conceive and then to implement. In my experience with Catalytica and from numerous successes I have seen elsewhere in the world, this approach is independent of a culture, and applies whether you are building a company in the United States, China, or the Czech Republic. We found the following eight "must haves" to be critical.

❖ Have a skilled CEO who embraces and is committed to Inspired Leadership, and has a deep sense of how to create a challenging, far-reaching, yet realistic company vision and mission. The CEO creates the dream; committed employees embrace and embellish it.[70]

❖ Achieve passionate buy-in of this vision and mission from all key stakeholders—customers, employees, investors, suppliers, and the community.

❖ Coach employees on developing corporate values to which they are firmly committed.

❖ Hire the *right people* for the *right positions* at the *right time*—and *compassionately* and *quickly* ask those to leave who do not work out.

❖ Address a *growing market*, better yet, create one!

❖ Focus strictly and passionately on the best opportunities. Plan for an *early commercial success*—even a modest one.

❖ Have a *strategic plan*, but stay flexible. For maximum effectiveness, the plan should be understood and embraced by all employees.

Catalytica as well as every successful enterprise that I have studied has had a healthy component of each of these eight principles. Let's look at each of them in more detail.

Qualities of a Skilled Leader

A skilled CEO is first and foremost a *servant*. His or her primary job is to determine how to duly serve each of the stakeholders, and to do so, he or she must develop a personal and a corporate strategy that creates whatever is necessary so that a fair return is consistently realized by all stakeholders. Sound corporate profit and stakeholder returns are not mutually exclusive. In fact, when properly executed such a strategy often maximizes profit. This was our experience at Catalytica.

A skilled CEO may seem like an obvious requirement. But, ask yourself, "What are the most important characteristics that form the basis for such servant leadership?" In my view, just as there are critical "must haves" to building a successful company, there are also fundamental *skills*, discussed in detail below, that taken together form the key elements of an *inspired leader*. It takes an inspired person to lead creation of the *soul* and *integrity* of the company. *First and foremost, the leader must be inspired by a vision, a mission, that is to say, a dream.* By the *soul*, I mean the culture, values, and spirit of the company all rolled up into one—analogous to what you might envision as the soul of a person. By integrity, I don't mean just honesty, but also the respect and consideration the company has for serving the "whole," i.e., employees, customers, vendors, community, humanity, and the planet. To accomplish this, a CEO should have or develop the following skills, and yes, they can be developed:

The CEO must actively inspire the company in the creation of and commitment to a compelling vision and mission—I would even say a "Corporate Dream" statement—and a challenging yet realistic strategy.

At Catalytica, our "Dream" was *to build a profitable company that helped create a sustainable world through clean, cost-effective technologies.* We wanted to help create a future for all the world's children, so that when they looked back in time they said, "Thank you!" and not, "Good lord, what were they thinking?" Although this "Dream" was created by my business partner and cofounder, Ricardo Levy, and me, all of our employees understood and were passionately committed to this "Dream." Literally everything we did of commercial value was driven by our "Dream." As will be discussed in chapter 7, this is similar to Lance Secretan's OneDream™ concept,[71] which emphasizes the fundamental requirement that all employees, better yet all *stakeholders*, understand and support the Dream.

Dreams move mountains and get things done. They have the power to change the world.

Rarely does the vision, mission, or dream emanate from a group of people. More often than not, they are formulated by the CEO. In business enterprises, they are often created by the founding entrepreneur, who may or may not be the CEO. However, the founder's Dream often attracts the right CEO to the company, and galvanizes his or her passion to help make this Dream a reality. He or she may even modify it to some degree, because in the end, the CEO must passionately own and live the Dream.

While the Dream may and often is set by the CEO, if employees are not involved in strategic refinements to achieve the Dream, and especially in developing the required tactics for their particular job, it is unlikely that there will be the level of commitment necessary to go the distance when times get tough—and they usually do get tough at one point or another. At Catalytica all employees enjoyed relating our story and our Dream. It is what enabled us to hire the very best people. Everyone wants to be part of a big Dream.

Although it is usually easy to follow a dynamic inspirational leader, charisma is not a primary requirement. Google's Eric Schmidt, Microsoft founder Bill Gates, and Berkshire Hathaway's Warren Buffet are all excellent leaders in their own ways, but none is considered charismatic.

The CEO must demonstrate, consistently in all actions, his or her passion for the company Dream.

And it must be authentic. Nothing excites people more than pure unbridled passion. My long-time business partner, Ricardo Levy, likes to say that the CEO must be "an engaging storyteller, one who conveys an authentic and convincing message, succeeds in infecting others with enthusiasm, and invites them to participate in the entrepreneurial dance. Most important, he or she must be fully committed."[72]

Have you ever had a conversation with someone concerning a subject for which you are completely unfamiliar, and find yourself deeply interested? You will subsequently find yourself asking, "How in the world did I ever develop an interest in this subject?" Most likely it was because the person you talked with had passion. Passion is contagious, because it creates a deep intimate connection of the spirit of one person with that of another. And when spirit is involved and the connection is made the commitment is intense and long-lasting. It's a fundamental principle of the way the universe functions.

The CEO must be tenacious to a fault, always encouraging the discovery of solutions to challenges and barriers along the way to the vision.

Recall what has become known as Churchill's shortest speech, *"Never, ever, ever, ever, ever, ever, ever, give in!"*[73] Of course, there are times when it's time to stop throwing good money after bad, and to terminate a project. The way an experienced leader makes this kind of decision is to truly listen to and to understand all of the pertinent data from all relevant participants, and then in a period of quiet meditation, to serve all of the stakeholders by making the final decision based on his or her personal intuition, which when properly cultivated, accessed, and used, is more powerful than all the computers you could possibly link together.

Discipline is an important attribute of successful and inspired leaders, especially in generating excellent returns for all stake-holders—not just the shareholders.

Here discipline means a clear, constant, and consistent commitment to agreed-upon goals and strategies. It is easy to get distracted in this world. The CEO's job is to be sure that everyone stays the course and deviates only when it is absolutely clear and necessary to do so.

An excellent leader knows how to inspire teams and employees in setting their values for the company.

This is not an easy task, and by no means should these values be only those of the CEO, although in the end, he or she must embrace them. Furthermore, I am not just speaking about knowing and practicing right from wrong, but more particularly, what is important to employees in doing their work? How do they want to work? What values would disturb them if violated, and which would motivate them when practiced by their management and fellow team members? It is best to do this when the company is small; it can be managed even for large organizations, but with much greater effort and commitment from the CEO.

In 2006 I went through this process with the first fifteen employees of my current enterprise, Chateau Mcely. The vision, mission, and dream for Chateau Mcely were set by my wife Inez and me. The corporate values were developed entirely by our employees under my facilitation and coaching. The final outcome is listed in Appendix C. As you read these values, please keep in mind that although I expressed the final statements in proper

English, the substance of each of these values was carefully crafted by fifteen Czech employees, some of whom at the time barely spoke English. All job interviewees and new employees are given a copy of these values and they are explained in detail to be sure they are clearly understood. At every corporate meeting, we consistently review these values to determine if they still hold for our employees and whether there is a need for refinement. In six years of operation, we have yet to make any changes.

Great leaders are compassionate.

They will walk through fire for their stakeholders and especially their employees. And there will be more than one occasion you will be asked to do so. At a deep level, an effective CEO or leader has a very special caring, I would even say love, for his or her employees. If this caring is balanced with all of the other criteria, you cannot help but have the most effective leader for the organization.

Allow me to share a story of compassion. In the mid-1990s, when Catalytica had set its strategy to enter the pharmaceutical business, we acquired from Sandoz, the Swiss pharmaceutical company, a small manufacturing plant located in East Palo Alto, California. Please note that East Palo Alto is not Palo Alto. It is located across the broad barrier divide of U.S. 101 from Palo Alto and is populated primarily by low-income African Americans and a Latino community. Unemployment was very high at the time.

I personally spent considerable time with then Supervisor Bill Vines and Mayor Rose Gibson to assure them and the supervisory board that we were an ecologically conscious operation, and more important we intended to work diligently to hire as many employees as possible from their community. We earnestly wanted to support East Palo Alto. Bill and Rose supported us and we eventually hired more than 90 percent of our plant operators from East Palo Alto. Most had a high school education or less, so we instituted an intense training program.

Shortly after the plant opened for Catalytica Pharmaceutical business, one of our operators, I will call him Jeff, was filling a metal drum with a flammable drug product. In his haste he ignored the critical safety requirement to connect the drum with a conducting wire to a ground to avoid any static electrical sparks from the liquid flowing into the drum. Subsequently, a static electrical spark was created and caused an explosion and a serious fire in the plant. Miraculously, neither Jeff nor anyone else was injured but the fire closed the plant for several weeks. Fortunately we had both fire and business-interruption insurance so we were able to pay our employees and we suffered minimal revenue losses.

The question then was, do we fire Jeff for violating our critical safety regulations and putting himself and others at serious risk? In discussions with our plant manager, Tom, I found out that Jeff was suffering from a significant personal issue at home. Tom suggested that we coach Jeff on how to approach the personal issue and get his firm, unwavering recommitment to safety for all future operations. Under the circumstances, I thought that Tom had a great idea. We implemented the plan and Tom's deep sense of compassion was not only felt by Jeff, who then became an excellent operator, but also by all of the other members of the plant team. Sincere compassion has great power!

In the end, the CEO must be an inspirational leader, not necessarily charismatic, but he or she must speak to and respect the hearts of the employees and the other stakeholders associated with the company.

Getting the Human Element Right

After having an inspired CEO, hiring the *right people* for the *right positions* at the *right time* is the second key ingredient in creating a successful company. It is one of the most difficult things to do correctly. In startup companies, entrepreneurs often hire friends, family, and others who may no longer be the right persons in their positions as the company grows. Or sometimes we are misled by the behavior of a candidate during the interview process. The leadership must face this reality and work with these employees to help them find a more effective and rewarding job within the company, and if one is not available then they should try in a compassionate way to find them a more rewarding position elsewhere. Everyone, including the employee, benefits by taking care of these issues sooner rather than later.

The first thing to do is to spend considerable effort in hiring the right person for the right job. This is not easy, and most companies falter in this area. At Catalytica we became known for our intense hiring techniques. We tried never to settle for a candidate if the individual was not the right person for the position, even when we were growing at double digit rates. Under the pressures of rapid growth, it is easy to settle by filling a position with someone who may not be the best candidate. We put together multidisciplinary teams to interview each candidate, whether it was for a position as a receptionist or the vice president of sales.

A list of key, open-ended questions was developed and each of the interview team members was assigned an area of focus for the candidate. Open-ended questions are very important and they assure you of a more truthful answer rather than what the candidate thinks you may want to hear, which is easy for them to do in specific focused inquiries. I want to hear the answers to such questions as "What are your personal dreams and aspirations?" "What's the most exciting thing that ever happened to you?" "What's the worst thing that ever happened to you, and how did you deal with it?" "What special skills do you believe you bring to our company and why would you want to work here?" The manner in which a candidate answers such open-ended questions will speak volumes about their capabilities and whether they fit your company values and the position you are trying to fill. We arranged at least one dinner with the candidate and then a dinner with the candidate and his or her significant other. Much can be gleaned from the candidate's behavior under these circumstances.

The interview team would then meet as a group and go over the answers to all questions and the candidate's behavior in a social setting. The input of a significant other can also be quite telling. The interview team would then vote on whether or not to hire the candidate and the results of the decision, with detailed comments, would be presented to the senior manager in the department for which the candidate was interviewing. In the end it is still a risky process, but we found our approach minimized the number of mistakes. However, when a mistake is made and an ineffective candidate is hired, what then?

A good leader never finds it easy to fire an employee. It is difficult to do. But if necessary, it is almost always in the best interest of both the company and the employee, as demonstrated in the following example.

When we first hired waiters for our restaurant at Chateau Mcely, one of our hires was an incredibly intelligent gentleman named Milan. He was only three weeks into his work with us when it became clear to our Food and Beverage Manager that Milan was not really passionate about his work and seemed to be distracted. Our Manager of Guest Relations told me that Milan seemed to spend a lot of time on the computer, and in fact was able to solve some of our difficult IT issues.

I had lunch with the Milan and asked him what he thought of his capabilities as a waiter. After hemming and hawing and a few false starts to his answer, it was clear that he really didn't love his job, and I pointed this out to him. He reluctantly agreed. I asked him if he ever thought about going into the computer business. Apparently not, though he had played with computers since childhood and could even repair them.

Although we were not legally required to do so because of the short duration of his tenure, we decided to give Milan four weeks' notice of termination, and told him that he could take off work whenever necessary for job interviews. I personally advised him to look for employment in the computer industry. Today, Milan is a successful computer technical serviceman for a large multinational company. I usually get a call or e-mail from him once or twice a year, thanking me for encouraging the move.

The Importance of Addressing a Growing Market

Entering a business to capture part of a stagnant market is a mistake, even if you do have better, more cost-effective technology. First of all, a minimal growth market is telling you something. This product or process is on its way out, and it's just a matter of time. So, why try to save it when there are so many other healthier ones that need help for growth.

At Catalytica we made this mistake—once! Based on our proprietary nanotechnology, we created a molecularly engineered catalyst that could provide a 10 percent yield increase in a commodity chemical product known as acetaldehyde used in the plastics and polymers industries. The catalyst was "nearly" a drop-in catalyst, meaning it required only a minimum amount of capital investment to be used in the existing manufacturing plant. We even carried out an expensive but successful pilot-plant test, which we paid for.

In the end our prospective customer, who confirmed the success of the pilot test, chose not to go forward with our technology. Why? Because our process required some capital investment, and the global demand for this commodity chemical was decreasing. It was clear that our potential customer, who had recovered all of his initial capital in the existing process, was simply going to ride out his "cash cow" until the demand for the product was so low that he could profitably shutter the plant, or modify it for the manufacture of a different product.

Contrast this with our successful efforts in pharmaceuticals, which at the time were growing at double digit rates. A growing market is so much more dynamic, so much more exciting, so much more forgiving, and has so many more possibilities. Don't waste your time on dying markets. Life is too short!

A Commitment to Focus

The need to focus cannot be overstated. Many "opportunities" will present themselves. With limited resources, the company cannot follow them all and succeed. The management team must pick the best commercial opportunities and galvanize the energy of the company behind them. One reason that companies often lose their focus is because product or process development is carried out in a linear fashion. For example, in the chemical industry a researcher will sometimes develop a laboratory process for a new product, only to find that when transferred to the engineering department the process to make the product cannot be scaled up economically. Or, if it gets that far, often detailed discussions in the marketplace show that there is not nearly the market that had been thought to exist, and, sometimes, there really is no market at all.

In such a non-achieving environment, you find various departments in the company losing perspective, commitment, and interest in the innovation process. Autonomous silos are at work! Therefore, you will find management representatives from various departments, including research, engineering, and commercial development, suggesting new ideas on which to work. "Yeah, I know we put several million dollars into Product A, but I have a better idea. Let's try Product B."

The way we minimized and eventually eliminated this problem at Catalytica was to form multidisciplinary teams from the very inception of a project. So, let's say that a scientist came up with an idea for making a new product that he or she felt had a good market. Immediately, someone from commercial development would establish whether or not this was correct, whether the market was growing, whether Catalytica could make an entry, what the barriers to entry were and how high, and what kind of returns we might expect if we were successful. Of course at this early stage much of this effort was based on "back-of-the-envelope" calculations.

If the idea passed this market test, we would then envision how the product would be made and do some preliminary engineering and process economic calculations. If it passed these barriers, and management thought that in view of all resource allocations we should proceed, a project team was formed with representation from *research, engineering,* and *commercial development.*

Initially, the team was led by a research scientist with input from the engineering and commercial development team members. As product development progressed, leadership switched to an engineer until the manufacturing process was designed and had assured scalability. Ultimately, with successful scale-up, the baton was passed to the commercial development participant who saw the project through to commercialization. The baton was passed in a ceremony at each stage. Everyone got the credit for further success. We started this kind of technological culture within Catalytica in the early 1980s when it was relatively unknown outside of our company. Today, it is more common to see this in industry. It required lots of patience and team building to change the culture of the people who joined Catalytica into this new way of thinking. But it worked well and was worth the effort.

Apple also eventually went to this same mode of operation. Subsequent to his ouster from Apple eleven years earlier, when Steve Jobs returned to that company in 1996 and found the company floundering and failing, he aggressively and intensely implemented focus. Many products were shut down in favor of the five major products that he felt would create a successful future for Apple. Furthermore, as a zealot for assuring successful product development and launches, he instituted the same multidisciplinary development strategy we had originated at Catalytica more than a decade earlier. Jobs put key members from product design, product development, manufacturing, and marketing on the same team. Initially the representatives from these four disciplines did not find it easy to work together, but in time this move was a key factor in the commercial success of the launches for the iPod, iPad, and iPhone products.

Targeting an Early Commercial Success

Having an early commercial success brings incredible benefits to a new company. Using our baseball analogy, hit a few singles instead of trying for all home runs. Early commercial success provides management with greater credibility and the company with higher valuations. A successful enterprise must continuously raise money for growth. With greater credibility and higher valuation, you give up less of your company with each round of financing.

We ran into this issue early on at Catalytica. We had raised about $80 million in venture capital, and although we were connected with excellent financial partners, and had apprised them of the lengthy time scale we needed to show commercial success, there was an unspoken pressure by the venture capitalists and some of our board members to pursue primarily "home runs." "Let's change the world in a big way," was the not-so-subliminal message. We were working on several projects, a success in any one of which would change the world.

When it became clear that we had spent a large level of funding and that commercial success might be a lot longer into the future than we had thought, we began to think of how we could hit a few singles. We iden ified the pharmaceutical industry as one which (a) was very profitable, (b) used manufacturing processes for which our expertise in catalytic science and engineering could make a big impact, and (c) was an untapped market with significant growth potential. This turned out to be a far greater signif cant strategic move than we had ever conceived.

We pulled together several key people from research, engineering, commercial development, and management. We identified a few small projects—"singles"—whose success gave us credibility and provided the launch pad to rapidly build a fully integrated pharmaceutical manufacturing company. With several immediate successes, Catalytica Pharmaceut cals, Inc. became the "lion's share" asset value of Catalytica. We acquired three manufacturing plants, and we began producing both prescription and over-the-counter drugs for many of the major multinational pharmaceutical companies. By "hitting a few singles" quickly, we raised the valuation of Catalytica so high that we were able to finance in a creative and reasonable fashion our astronomical growth.

Have a Plan, but Stay Flexible

It is important to have a plan, but having flexibility is critical. To give an example, our strategic plan for Catalytic Pharmaceuticals was based on our initial mission: *to become a leading multinational supplier of interme-diates and bulk active ingredients for the pharmaceutical industry.* Inter-mediates are special chemical compounds that are used to manufacture the bulk active ingredient for a final drug. The bulk active ingredient is the actual active component in the drug. As a simple example, salicylic acid is an intermediate used to make acetylsalicylic acid, which is the bulk active ingredient in aspirin. The actual aspirin tablet has a number of additional components that provide tablet integrity, rate of uptake in the bloodstream, and other key therapeutic actions. Manufacturing the final packaged drug is a very different level of commitment and complexity than producing intermediates and bulk active ingredients.

When Catalytica Pharmaceuticals reached annual revenues of almost $20 million based on our plant in East Palo Alto, we decided we needed to obtain a second manufacturing plant. Over a period of eighteen months we looked at five plants all over North and South America, with no success. Then in 2005 we encountered a unique opportunity. Back in 1995, Glaxo Pharmaceuticals merged with Burroughs Wellcome Pharmaceuticals, and subsequently in 2000 they merged with SmithKlineBeecham. As is the custom with mergers and acquisitions, there was a planned "rationalization" of the new entities. By the mid-1990s GlaxoWellcome and its management team decided they had to shed a couple of their manufacturing plants. Since Glaxo is a British company, for political reasons they chose not to do so in the United Kingdom.

This meant that Wellcome's premiere plant in Greenville, North Carolina would come on the market. We were quite excited because they had an excellent intermediates and bulk actives manufacturing facility. I immediately flew to North Carolina and expressed our Company's interest, but after a tour of the plant, it was clear that this incredible facility was a fully integrated manufacturing plant, starting from basic chemical ingredients and ending up with the final packaged drugs, which could then be shipped anywhere in the world. The plant was even capable of producing its own packaging materials. Furthermore, the facility had a fully-integrated sterile manufacturing plant, which was by far the best in North America. This meant it could produce injectable drugs as well as a host of high-value-added drugs that required optimal sterility for their manufacture. Manufacturing pharmaceuticals that require a sterile facility is very challenging, but also very profitable.

There was no way we could buy only a piece of the plant, and so after discussions with our management team and our board, we decided that the opportunity was too good to pass. Such a move would thrust us into the entire pharmaceutical manufacturing spectrum, well beyond our then stated mission. We had several critical board meetings to discuss our options and after receiving significant perspectives from the "giants" on our board, in particular Ernest Mario, who was formerly CEO of Glaxo, we decided to go forward with the acquisition.

Rather than stop us, the addition increased our scope of opportunities, and our mission changed to *becoming a leading global pharmaceutical manufacturer.* We competed successfully with five multibillion-dollar companies for this acquisition. How we succeeded is another story in itself. However, it was this acquisition that transformed us from a modest small company to an operation with annual revenues of $375 million, ultimately growing to nearly $500 million before selling the company at a significant premium, bringing a great return not just to our shareholders, but to all of our stakeholders. Flexibility was one of the key elements enabling us to make this decision.

* * *

A Call to Action

The twenty-first century has presented humanity with some of the greatest challenges since its very genesis. For example, every month that goes by, we fill in more of the technological puzzle concerning climate change and the picture looks increasingly grim. An increase in the average global temperature of 2° C by the end of the century appears unavoidable, 3°–4° C is more likely, and 6° C is a possibility, but we dare not consider the upper value of this seemingly modest 6° C temperature increase, as it will mean the end of humanity as we know it.

The other side of the climate change "coin" is global energy security, which has placed the world in one of the most dangerous political and economic positions in its history. Poverty and disease in developing nations are rampant as ever, and healthcare challenges in developed countries seem beyond comprehension. All of this has led to political unrest and what appear to be untenable situations in North Korea, Afghanistan, Pakistan, Iran, Iraq, Libya, Syria, Sudan, Somalia, Venezuela, and elsewhere. The Western World appears to be at odds in various economic and political arenas with China and Russia. Energy security is a major factor in this political unrest.

All of these as well as other related global challenges can be addressed by one strategic approach: INNOVATION—innovation in the way we conduct politics; innovation in the way we create and manage economic models; innovation in the way we manufacture, sell, and distribute products and services; and innovation in the way in which we deal with critical social issues such as poverty, healthcare, and education. After all, what is innovation but the confluence of physical, financial, and intellectual resources—people, financing, ideas, and concepts—in a novel manner to solve problems in the marketplace for the purpose of creating added value and delivering a fair return to all stakeholders.

Profit in our new way of thinking should be much more than a financial return on investment. Equally important, our strategy should include a social return as well. They need not be mutually exclusive. In the long run, a lack of social return precipitates the problems mentioned above, and worse. As discussed in chapter 4, the Bhutanese have developed and practice a model of productivity that is not measured by a conventional Gross National Product (GNP), but by Gross National Happiness (GNH). It features four pillars (economy, culture, environment, and governance), nine domains (psychological well-being, ecology, health, education, culture, living standards, time use, community vitality, and governance), and seventy-two indicators of happiness—and the Bhutanese are quite serious about its use as a measure of progress. I am not suggesting that this model is necessarily the best one, but it is, in my opinion, in the right direction. The GDP model has run its course and is no longer an effective means to a safe and sustainable humanity.

The kind of innovation we should contemplate and pursue should create jobs, stimulate economic and social growth, assure global sustainability, and provide a means to world peace. To do this, we need to set a value on quality of life and not just on goods and services. There has been much research on practical ways and incentives to do this. Now is the time to implement these recommendations.[74] What is required is that one or more of the great nations of this world set an example by moving in this direction. Others will follow as they see the economic and social benefits. I don't think governments will provide the leadership, but they can and must provide the right environment and legal and financial stimuli.

Business, now the most powerful and influential force on the planet, must provide the inspirational vision, mission, values, and the dream. It's in its best interest. This means creating successful companies that embrace this philosophy. They should be led by inspired leaders who know how to ignite the passions of people, a fundamental necessity for innovation and success on all levels of business and social structures.

In a word, there has never been a greater opportunity to create and innovate through inspired leadership. What a wonderful time to be an inspired business leader! All that is necessary is for a few leaders to step forward and have the courage to show us the way. I offer you this "Dream"—*"A peaceful, just, and sustainable world for all our children."*

CHAPTER 7

Inspirational Leadership®: Inspire Self – Others – The World

There is a growing movement that seeks to restore joy, significance, and personal worth in work and life. It is a movement formed by leaders who are leaving old ideas of leadership behind and adopting new philosophies that inspire others to get things done and to live meaningful and fulfilling lives.[75]

—LANCE SECRETAN

KEY CONCEPTS

❖ The most effective means of organizational leadership is rapidly evolving to a new way of *thinking* and *being* in order to manage the global challenges and opportunities of an increasingly complex and interconnected society.

❖ Inspirational Leadership®,[76] created and popularized by Dr. Lance Secretan, succinctly portrays and embraces this transition.

❖ Inspirational Leadership is based on the CASTLE Principles™, an acronym for *Courage, Authenticity, Service, Truthfulness, Love, and Effectiveness.*[77] When internalized and practiced proficiently, these principles form the basis for creating an organization that is personally rewarding, commercially advantageous, and socially responsible.[78] It makes the world a much better place in which to live.

The Leadership Evolution

There has probably been more written over the ages about leadership than any other subject in the business arena. For our purpose, I would prefer to keep things simple and to the point, and focus only on the fundamental aspects of leadership that are critical for building a better world, which are the same principles necessary to build an enduring successful business.

To my way of thinking there are three broad types of leadership. The first is *Leadership via Fear and Threat.* An example would be living and functioning in Nazi Germany during the Second World War, especially if you were Jewish or a member of one of the constituencies that Adolph Hitler considered a threat to his Aryan plan. "Successful" leaders of this type were practiced at demonstrating horrible consequences to those who did not follow orders. This kind of leadership presents zero possibilities for creativity and innovation, as followers must implement specific orders to the letter or face a terrible fate. *The degree of creativity is directly related to the level of uncertainty. When things are specific or certain there is no room for creativity.*

The second general form of leadership is *Leadership via Reward.* This is sometimes called the "Carrot and Stick" model. If you perform well and meet the goals I set for you, you get a reward, and if you don't, you not only don't get a reward, you might even suffer a loss, such as your job. This form of leadership, although not nearly as harsh as the *Fear and Threat* model, is still primarily focused on achieving goals that are important to the leader.

The third form of leadership is *Inspired Leadership*, sometimes called *Conscious Leadership.* Inspired leadership has been studied, refined, and more fully developed by Lance Secretan who refers to it as *Inspirational Leadership*® and it is the subject of this chapter. As you will see, this kind of leadership does not require designation, promotion, or anointing of a specific individual. Anyone can be an "inspirational leader." In a word, inspirational leaders have found out who they are, why they are here, and they are dedicated to making this a better world by following their passion, a powerful magnetic force based on their innate and cultivated skills and goals.

As I stressed in chapter 6, an inspirational leader need not be charismatic. What an inspirational leader does is more important to those being inspired than his or her personality dynamics. Yes, it is a plus if employees can feel the personal "energy" of a leader, but this is not a central requirement. In the end, actions trump verbal promises and even personal charismatic energy.

I have seen this kind of subtle impact of inspired leadership over and over again. I recall that while working for Exxon, a charismatic technical manager was transferred from our research center in New Jersey to an Exxon research facility in Baton Rouge, Louisiana. He was a good manager, well liked and to some degree he inspired the members of his team. His replacement had a more relaxed personality; he certainly was not charismatic.

The team members were at first quite disappointed. However, over the ensuing months the new manager showed his effectiveness. For example, he was successful in convincing Exxon's executive management of the wisdom in purchasing two expensive pieces of research equipment, something the prior manager had tried to do several times but was unsuccessful. These purchases afforded the team several key scientific discoveries and important technical and legal support for a number of new patents that built on and protected Exxon's commercial intellectual property rights in polymers and petrochemicals. They also resulted in several prestigious, internationally-recognized scientific papers. The new manager eventually became a prized possession of the team members and of the Exxon management.

To be sure, there is a broad spectrum of subcategories within each of these three designations, and in certain instances, even within the category of *Leadership by Fear and Threat* there can be some value. For example, a young, inexperienced infantry soldier kneeling in a foxhole may be threatened by his stern squad leader to "Keep your damned head down before it gets shot off!" That works just fine.

But as Lance Secretan and other supporters of *Inspirational Leadership* have demonstrated, the power of this form of leadership can foster the accomplishment of incredibly challenging tasks, it builds character in the leader and those being "led," and it can change the world for the better, even under the most dire circumstances.

I focus here on the principles of *Inspirational Leadership* developed by Lance Secreatan. I have found that they most closely describe and complement many of the principles that my colleagues and I at Catalytica found to work for us over years of trial and error. As mentioned earlier, we called it *Inspired Leadership* because we found that only deeply inspired leaders could truly inspire others. They remained the same effective principles even as we grew our company from a small entrepreneurial enterprise to a successful manufacturing company of nearly 2,000 people. Furthermore, Lance has packaged these principles in a neat structure that is readily accessible to anyone working in a business or building a company. However, I will reiterate that these same principles enable anyone to live a more conscious and inspirational life, and therefore to have a very positive impact on the world around them. They apply not only to managers and CEOs, but also to mothers, fathers, spiritual leaders, politicians, and others. Anyone can choose to be an Inspirational Leader; it does not require a promotion.

Historically, *Leadership via Fear and Threat* was the primary mode of directing the growth of business starting with the Industrial Revolution in the mid-eighteenth century and up through the end of the Second World War. About that time, business in the developed world began a serious transition to *Leadership via Reward*. However, over the last decade as the developed world has come face-to-face with what are often thought of as insurmountable global challenges, there has been a movement toward *Inspirational Leadership*. Its principles are the ways of long-lasting and successful enterprises such as IBM, FedEx, Amazon, UPS, Starbucks, Proctor & Gamble, Patagonia, Google, and many more. A not insignificant force behind this transition has been a definite trend toward higher levels of consciousness among a large fraction of people in both the developing and developed world.

The Power of Inspiration

Have you ever worked with a person who inspired your professional and personal endeavors so deeply that you just might have considered working for minimum wage? I have. It is a most exhilarating experience, and it's as personally rewarding and professionally fulfilling as it gets!

As I conveyed in my own story, my first job after graduate school was as a research scientist with Exxon. Prior to my full-time employment with Exxon, and during the summer of my last year as a PhD candidate in physical chemistry at Rutgers University in New Jersey, I was accepted as a summer research associate working for the late Dr. John H. Sinfelt at Exxon Research & Engineering Co. In retrospect, this move provided excellent experience for my entrepreneurial adventures that would follow. Should you be inclined to start your own entrepreneurial enterprise, working first in a quality large company that operates in your chosen field of endeavor can result in significant educational benefits. You can get a sense of the real world and that will enable you to better understand what you must do if you want to make it a better place in which to live.

My experience in R&D with a premier company such as Exxon and especially with John, a world-famous scientist and commercial technologist, developed my background in commercial technologies and, therefore, my professional credibility. My move to California was not to be for another seven years. I would be captured by the talent and technical genius of John Sinfelt, who, equally importantly, was gifted with the capability of elevating the human spirit. That is what inspiration is all about. Although not what most might call charismatic, John was unquestionably a true Inspirational Leader.

I didn't realize at the time that John was one the world's most accomplished scientists in the important field of catalysis. Catalytic industrial processes are directly responsible for more than 30 percent of our annual global GDP—everything from fuels to food to fibers and pharmaceuticals. And beyond that, enzymes—natural biocatalysts—are the unique force that helped create life on our planet and orchestrate all of our bodily processes from the moment of conception to the instant of death—and actually, for some time afterwards, as well!

John had been nominated for the Nobel Prize, and had won more honors in science than most in his field. When I entered his office for the first time and addressed him as Dr. Sinfelt, his immediate response was "Call me John, please." I found him to be brilliant, yet humble. He could explain complex technical concepts so clearly and accurately that even a non-technical person could understand them. He was thorough, careful, and deeply considerate of his coworkers. I suppose you could say that John was very comfortable with who he was and what he was doing with his life. He had a quiet passion for his work, and yet he could be as determined "as a bulldog" to reach his goals, once he had the internal commitment to do so.

I learned so much from John about science, technology, people, and about life. But most of all, he inspired me to be the best I could be at everything I did. He was one of the giants in my life and standing on his shoulders gave me a view of technology and of my future that I could never have gotten anywhere else. This dream job was such a gift that I would indeed have worked there for minimum wage!

What are the fundamental principles that underpin inspirational people like John? Are they born that way? Do they learn these principles along the way? What gives them purpose, passion, and more fundamentally, *what causes them to bring out the best in the people around them—to inspire people to actualize their best personal potential?* I have asked these questions many times. I think one person who has found the answers is Lance Secretan.

As Lance points out, what he terms Inspirational Leadership is not just the purview of the CEO or management. If the climate and culture are right within an organization, anyone can assume an inspirational leader's role; and that can have profound positive consequences for the organization. As mentioned later in this chapter, I have seen this firsthand with the teams at Catalytica and more recently with the teams at Chateau Mcely.

Lance's qualifications are noteworthy. As a former CEO of Manpower, Inc., the world's largest employer, he helped lead that enterprise to a multi-billion-dollar FORTUNE 200 company. Lance subsequently launched a successful venture called The Secretan Center, a global consulting practice specializing in cultural and leadership transformation to achieve extraordinary improvements in personal and organizational performance. He is the author of fifteen books on leadership, including his best seller *The Spark, the Flame and the Torch: Inspire Self. Inspire Others. Inspire the World*.[79] His clients include thirty of FORTUNE Magazine's "America's Most Admired Companies" and twelve of the "100 Best Companies to Work for in America." His premise is that organizations that have operated so successfully in the challenging global commercial climate, which has been growing in intensity over the last two decades have moved to a higher level of leadership—a quantum jump—from Motivational Leadership, the old style of directing employees to achieve the leader's agenda, to the concepts of Inspirational Leadership. He maintains that this movement is a natural evolution of the human psyche to enable us to manage the global complexities and challenges of a diverse, interconnected world.

Inspirational Leadership®

So, what is Inspirational Leadership, especially as it applies to the corporate world? What sets it apart from conventional leadership approaches? We can summarize the key aspects of Inspirational Leadership by looking at what Inspirational Leaders do.

They do the following:

❖ Build businesses that benefit all stakeholders—employees, customers, investors, suppliers, and society.

❖ Fervently internalize and pursue their company's purpose—vision, mission, dream, values, goals, and strategies—and enthusiastically and effectively communicate this purpose to all of the company's stakeholders and how it will benefit all of them.

❖ Create an environment that inspires employees to passionately direct their personal and professional skills at the company's purpose, while simultaneously enhancing their own capabilities.

Just how do these leaders do this? Can Inspirational Leadership be learned? The answer to the second question is "Absolutely!" As to the "how," Lance summarizes the important elements in what he calls the CASTLE Principles™—*Courage, Authenticity, Service, Truthfulness, Love, and Effectiveness*. When followed faithfully, he maintains that "These principles are the path to becoming free of living small, uninspiring lives, enabling us instead to live bright lives as a flame that lights the way for others, making a difference and lifting their spirits." He and his colleagues at The Secretan Center, Inc. have developed an effective organizational tool that accurately measures the degree to which employees feel that their company is practicing the CASTLE Principles. What is so special about Inspirational Leadership is that anyone in the organization can assume this role. It is not necessary to be anointed, appointed, or promoted. However, it is critical that the corporate culture permit and support this behavior, which means that the CEO and senior managers must be Inspirational Leaders.

Courage

> *Courage is what it takes to stand up and speak; courage is also what it takes to sit down and listen.*[80]
>
> —Winston Churchill

Inspiring leaders practice mental and moral courage, always following their basic personal values and the values of the organizations they lead. This becomes part of their operational fabric; they know that most people have a disdain for cowards and admire people and leaders with courage. And this admiration almost always flows from a deep-seated trust in the courageous leader.

Lance Secretan is a certified ski instructor, and as such, he often uses skiing as a metaphor and tool for teaching Inspirational Leadership. It is an integral part of some of the courses he teaches at the Secretan Center, high in the rugged Rocky Mountains of Colorado. In his book, *The Spark, the Flame, and the Torch,* he points out that he regularly accomplishes what many ski instructors say is impossible—he enables leadership students of intermediate skiing ability to overcome their fears so that they ski moguls during their first half day and double-black diamond runs ("experts only" terrain) by the end of the first day.[81]

He does this by gaining their trust, expertly evaluating their true capabilities, which are generally much beyond their internal perception, and challenging them to personal feats they thought not possible. This is primarily because as with many leaders, they have reached a plateau in their internal perception of their potential, and they continue to coast. They fail to realize that they can do much better. This is a general misperception that many of us face: we can always do much more mentally and physically than we ever dreamed of!

During one of his leadership courses, Lance and a group of executives were at the top of a 12,500-foot mountain in Colorado. The weather unexpectedly changed to a snowstorm with nearly zero visibility, known to mountaineers as a "whiteout." Lance told the skiers—all with early intermediate skills—that the only way off this very steep peak, which he knew like the back of his hand, was for them to trust him and descend single file following the backs of his skis. They did so, and all made it down safely without incident. The skiers trusted Lance because he had already demonstrated that he cared for them and would not put them in unnecessary danger; they saw his commitment throughout the week's course to help them grow as leaders; and because he never accepted any of their unjustified fears.[82] This was a true balance of compassion with trust in and knowledge of human potential. Caring leads to trust where it is possible to let go of uncertainties. This leads to change, and in change there is power.

As Lance reminds us, "It takes little courage to cling to the stillness of the status quo—it is movement and change, which involve letting go of the familiar while embracing the new, that requires courage. In this way, we sacrifice what we are for what we can become—and that takes courage."[83] He quite rightly points out that it takes courage to do those things that we admire in great leaders: being vulnerable; admitting a mistake; the ability to apologize sincerely; showing others that we care for them; listening to understand, and not just to hear; empathizing; abandoning flawed decisions; changing ways that no longer serve us well; and standing for integrity. Doing any of these inspires those around us.

I have enjoyed high-altitude mountain climbing over the years and I have found that it takes at least as much courage to inspire people as it does to climb challenging peaks, and the elation with success far exceeds that in conquering even the highest peaks. As Irish novelist and poet, C. S. Lewis was fond of saying, "Courage is not simply one of the virtues, but the form of every virtue at the testing point."

Authenticity

Being authentic is, first knowing yourself, then being yourself.
Authenticity derives from our deepest, truest selves. How do
we come to know ourselves? Only through what can be called
spiritual disciplines: silence, meditation, prayer.[84]

—JAMES A. AUTRY

Authenticity is alignment of what we do with what we think and say. Mahatma Gandhi used to say that we are authentic when what we think, say, and do are all the same. This builds trust in those around us. One of the hallmarks of authenticity is the ability to admit mistakes. So often in the corporate world, there is a tendency to not accept responsibility for mistakes. In fact, there is sometimes an effort to place the blame elsewhere. There is fear of reprisal, punishment, and the appearance of incompetence.

Two tragedies come to my mind that illustrate the power of authenticity in corporate leadership. The first is the Three Mile Island (TMI) nuclear accident which occurred in 1979 near Harrisburg, Pennsylvania. It is the most significant accident in the history of the American nuclear industry. The plant was owned and operated by General Public Utilities and Metropolitan Edison Company. Through a series of human errors, a partial core meltdown occurred in one of its pressurized-water nuclear reactors, releasing thirteen million curies of moderately potent radioactive gases and twenty curies of especially dangerous radioactive iodine-131 isotope. A curie is a unit of radioactivity equivalent to the amount of radioactive material that decays at the rate of 37 billion disintegrations per second. It is approximately equivalent to the radioactivity from 1 gram of radium and has the potential to cause cancer and leukemia.

Information released by the operating companies was confusing and often incorrect and misleading. To this day, the potential health impact on living species is still debated. As a consequence, the incident created a huge negative reaction that gave birth to a strong anti-nuclear movement, which led to the decline of the American nuclear industry. Although the impact of this accident was not minimal as the plant owners contended, it is now generally thought that the impact on them and the nuclear industry could have been exponentially less negative had they been forthright with the public and admitted certain wrongdoing, even if it had resulted in litigation. The companies would have come out ahead and the United States nuclear industry would most likely not have suffered such decline. Their misfortunate fate was a consequence of the antithesis of Inspirational Leadership, what you might call Repressive Leadership.

Contrast the TMI incident with handling of the disastrous Chicago Tylenol murders, which occurred in 1982. Seven people died after taking the pain-relief drug, which someone had laced with potassium cyanide. The management team at Johnson & Johnson, the pharmaceutical firm that manufactures Tylenol®, took immediate responsibility by working openly and accurately with the authorities to determine how this could have happened. Although one man was charged and imprisoned for trying to extort $1 million from Johnson & Johnson, he was never found guilty of poisoning the victims by tampering with bottles of Tylenol in various Chicago pharmacies.

Johnson & Johnson became a textbook case on how to deal authentically with a corporate disaster, and the company received significant positive coverage by the media for its handling of the crisis. The *Washington Post* reported that "Johnson & Johnson has effectively demonstrated how a major business ought to handle a disaster. This is no Three Mile Island accident in which the company's response did more damage than the original accident." The newspaper applauded the company for being honest with the public. In addition to instantly issuing a recall on Tylenol, Johnson & Johnson established direct links with the Chicago Police, the FBI, and the Food and Drug Administration.[85]

Does authenticity in leadership pay off? At the time of the crisis the Tylenol share of the analgesic market collapsed from 35 percent to 8 percent, but it rebounded in less than a year, which was credited with Johnson & Johnson's prompt, honest, open, and aggressive actions. The company reintroduced Tylenol with a triple-sealed, tamper-proof packaging, and coupled with price promotions, within a short time Tylenol became the most popular over-the-counter analgesic medicine in U.S. history. Their creative packaging solution also became the global safety gold standard for protecting the public from future incidents with other bottled products. In contrast to the TMI incident, the success of Tylenol after such an incredible crisis was the result of a management versed in and totally committed to authenticity.[86]

Service

> ...*Recognize that prosperity and happiness can be*
> *obtained only through honest service.*[87]
>
> —HENRY FORD

Albert Einstein was an avowed atheist and yet considered a spiritual person as well. How could this be? He was an atheist because he did not believe in God as defined by organized religions. He was spiritual in the sense that he did believe in an unknown and as yet undefined "Force" or entity—perhaps a "First Force"—that permeates the cosmos and is responsible for, and hopefully could explain, all physical and nonphysical phenomena.[88] He spent the largest part of his professional life at the Institute for Advanced Study in Princeton, New Jersey, trying to unify his Theory of General Relativity with quantum physics in hopes that he just might get a sense for this entity. Today, some of the most renowned physicists are still looking to discover this "First Force." They call their quest the search for the "Theory of Everything."

Although Einstein was one of the founding fathers of quantum physics, he thought it was an incomplete theory with "hidden variables" as yet undiscovered by science, and which once uncovered would explain all of the apparently "mystical" quantum phenomena that permeate our universe.[89] Perhaps this is what he meant when he is claimed to have said, "I want to know the mind of God; the rest are just details."

If you dig further into Einstein's philosophy and science, it is no surprise to find that he felt the fundamental purpose of life is service. It is claimed that he said *"Only a life lived for others, is a life worthwhile."* In a similar way, John William Gardner, author of *On Leadership*, Secretary of Health, Education and Welfare under U.S. President Lyndon B. Johnson, President of the Carnegie Corporation and founder of *Common Cause* and *Independent Sector*, has a quotation often attributed to him: *"When people are serving, life is no longer meaningless."* And as the quote at the beginning of this section succinctly notes, even successful corporate titans such as Henry Ford, founder of the Ford Motor Company, recognized the power and potential of service.

Why is it that wise thinkers and highly successful people such as Einstein, Gardener, Ford, and many others all came to this common conclusion—*Life is all about service*? There is strong evidence that they ultimately concluded that all people, and in fact all things in the universe, are to varying degrees connected.[90] Service recognizes that this interconnectedness or oneness provides a powerful synergy, and the possibility of a great return to all stakeholders. When I help you, I help myself, as well.

By example, I offer my experience as the owner of Chateau Mcely the former rural manor of the famous Thurn-Taxis aristocratic family, whose fortune came by founding the postal system in Europe during the Middle Ages. In 2006, the year that total renovation was completed and Chateau Mcely opened for business, it won first place in the "Best of Realty" for sensitive restoration of a heritage property. Subsequently it was voted by the World Travel Organization as the "World's Leading Green Hotel," and recently was voted by the same group as the "Best SPA in the Czech Republic."

The Chateau Mcely team, currently led by Founding Managing Director, Vlastimil Plch, and his management team, embraces and summarizes its professional sense of purpose and *service* as follows:

OUR VISION:
To make a difference in the world by making a positive difference in the lives of our guests and fellow teammates.

OUR MISSION:
To support our guests and teammates towards their highest personal potential with an environment that balances body, mind, and spirit.

OUR PROMISE:
To provide our guests with the highest level of service and comfort.

OUR PICTURE:
A cozy, relaxed, friendly atmosphere with the service of a leading, five-star hotel.

OUR DREAM:
To create a better world by enriching the lives of our guests and employees.

OUR VALUES:[91]
We continuously surprise our guests.
We practice integrity and mutual respect in all that we do.
We seek and appreciate feedback from our teammates and our guests.

We seek the Joy of Life for our guests, our teammates, and ourselves.

We solve challenging problems together.

We are a learning organization.

We focus on the Triple Bottom Line—People, Planet, Profit.

We work as a family.

I want to note, very importantly, that only our vision and mission were developed by the executive management team. Our promise, our picture, our dream, and our values, were developed by our employees. They are reviewed every year by the employees and have essentially remained the same since we opened Chateau Mcely.

By embracing and following the above vision, mission, and values, the Chateau Mcely team demonstrates its commitment to serve all stakeholders. Perhaps this is why a visit to the discriminating, online travel guide TripAdvisor at www.TripAdvisor.Com, shows at this moment in time, that of one hundred and five reviews, ninety-four are rated as Excellent and nine as Very Good. These reviews are unprecedented for most luxury hotels, which is why you will see the following guest quotes among them: *"An absolutely wonderful experience!"—"The most relaxing and carefree weekend I've ever had!"—"A great place to relax with an amazing staff!"—"Chateau Mcely—the best five-star hotel I've stayed in!"—"Exquisitely conscious and comfortable on all levels!"*

These accolades and awards do not happen by accident. They also do not result from Chateau Mcely necessarily having cornered the most talented staff in the Czech Republic—although, to be sure, they are intelligent, capable, and personable. This outcome is based on conscientious hard work and a total commitment to **service** throughout the organization. Vlastimil Plch and his management team work with each of the team members from the moment of their employment and thereafter. Employees build their commitment to service by Chateau Mcely providing them with the most effective tools to do their job well, and an environment that fosters their personal and professional growth. This enables them to most effectively serve our guests, their fellow team members, our community, and, in fact, all of the stakeholders connected to the Chateau Mcely adventure.

We do this by minimizing all forms of internal competition, which we see as the antithesis of **service.** We support a culture where team members listen to understand and not just to hear each other. Most business partnerships and even marriages fall apart when there is no longer a focus on listening with understanding and compassion.

At Chateau Mcely there is no fear of retribution for mistakes, and this component of our environment is reinforced by Vlastimil, who does not hesitate to admit to his own mistakes or to change course when one of his decisions is found to be ineffective. There is a sense of compassion, family, and sharing. We build on this sense of service by demonstrating trust We disclose to all employees our financial goals and progress and at the end of the year we share with them a significant fraction of our profit. In many ways, many of the Chateau Mcely team members become inspirational leaders in their own right. It's not just a management thing.

All of this is not to say that Chateau Mcely is without its personnel challenges. We have had our share of them. Although we work intersely to try to hire the right person for the right job at the right time, we some-times make mistakes. We try to minimize these challenges by an extensive interview process and testing by an outside human resource firm. It's in the best interest of Chateau Mcely and the interviewing candidate. When we do make a mistake, the person hired usually feels uncomfortable in our environment and leaves of his or her own accord. Or, the employee feels pressure from other members of the team, and decides to leave. If neither of these mechanisms occurs, we counsel the employee in a most compassionate manner to find another employer, one who more closely fits the employee's skills and needs. Commitment to service has an incredibly powerful force. Employees are fostered and enlightened into a creative stance that enables them to solve challenging problems, work extremely efficiently, and develop an increasing commitment to all corporate stakeholders. *Service* is unquestionably one of the strongest indicators of a highly effective and accomplished enterprise and its leadership.

Truthfulness

> *The truth in you remains as radiant as a star, as pure as light, as innocent as love itself. And you are worthy that your will be done.*[92]
>
> —HELEN SCHUCMAN

It's difficult, and often disappointing or embarrassing, to ***always*** tell the truth. Ultimately, however, telling the truth imbues in the teller an unparalleled power of persuasion and strength, and in the listener, unwavering commitment to the teller. This is because, deep down, we all seek unconditional trust and truth and it's not easy to find. Just read the political news or turn on the television. In contrast, I am continually amazed by and learn from my six-year old Julia, who like most children her age, always "tells it like it is!"

My wife, Inez, and I were recently invited by movie producer friends to the world premiere of a much anticipated film by a new director. In my truthful opinion, after viewing the film, I felt it was "okay," at best. We attended the premier party afterwards, and I was dreading the moment when someone might ask me what I thought of the film. How do you tell the truth without hurting those involved in making the film? The answer, of course, is that you can't. But not telling the truth often hurts them more in the long run.

Then it happened. One of the producers approached me and asked, "Well Jim, what did you think?" I nearly froze with my words, but knew that I had to respond, and I wanted to do so truthfully. "Look," I said, "I was in the film business for a brief stint of my professional journey, but I was blessed with incredible people around me to have the good fortune that occurred with *What Matters Most,* my first and only feature film. So, I'm really not a good judge of the quality of the film." I rapidly scanned my memory for those aspects of the film that I honestly felt were quite good, and then continued, "I think the acting and the camera work were very good. The subject matter of the script is of limited interest to me, so in total, I was not overly impressed. But, I'm probably in the minority; perhaps others will find it to be fine film."

My producer friend made it abundantly clear that I *was* the minority and that everyone he spoke with "loved the film." But, as I found out later by speaking with others at the party, this was not the case; most people simply did not want to hurt his feelings. Unfortunately, that's how our modern world moves. I doubt that we will ever be invited to another premier by my producer friend! As a postscript, and certainly not based on my critique, the film did poorly in the theaters.

In preparing material for his book, *One: The Art and Practice of Conscious Leadership*, Lance Secretan found that extensive research shows that people in general tell on average thirteen lies per week, and that lying occurs in nearly two-thirds of our interpersonal conversations. Furthermore, about 75 percent of professionals "pump up" their resumes, and between 20 and 30 percent of business managers have written fraudulent internal reports.[93] But that's not how great organizations work, those led by inspirational leaders.

Inspirational Leaders, regardless of whether it's challenging or not to tell the truth, are intimately aware that the single most reliable predictor of employee productivity and satisfaction is **TRUST!** It is a definite competitive advantage in business. In my experience, inspirational leaders understand the ways to cultivate trust in their organization:

❖ They excite all of their stakeholders with their vision and mission for the company.

❖ Employees must understand, and to some degree, participate in developing the company's strategy—at least that part which applies to the successful accomplishment of their efforts.

❖ Employees must intimately understand how their role can contribute to achieving the company's goals.

❖ They share with employees the company's progress and how their team is doing relative to their team goals as well as to the company goals, and do so with impeccable honesty.

Inspirational Leaders create highly effective, competitive organizations and a stimulating creative environment in which to work. They understand that trust brings out the best in people. As a result, employees see themselves as "bigger than life," and they work that way. They also make our world a better place.

Love

> *There is only one happiness in this life, to love and be loved.*[94]
>
> —GEORGE SAND

"Use the word 'love' in a business environment—are you crazy?" That's the normal reaction by executives schooled in the old business model—the Motivational Model. The problem emanates from the fact that in the English language, we use one word for love to serve many meanings, while in Sanskrit there are ninety-six words, eighty in Persian, and three in Greek that define different kinds of love. Therefore, in English, "love" can mean a broad spectrum of feelings and attitudes ranging from a simple pleasure such as "I loved that meal," to a platonic state of being, "I love the way she dresses," to intense interpersonal attachment such as, "I love her with my whole heart and soul."

From a philosophical point of view, love can also be seen as a virtue, where one extols a sense of compassion, caring, and kindness. Consequently we find that in much of the Western world, this diversity of meanings for the word "love" often causes confusion and makes it difficult to define and to communicate what is truly meant in a given situation. However, love is perhaps the most important psychological concept and force in any culture. In its various forms, it is the prime facilitator in all interpersonal relationships and has the most significant power to make things happen. It matters not whether the relationship is a compassionate one based on business, or a passionate connection with your lover. Love is the ultimate force field!

Therefore, it cannot be eliminated from the business arena if one expects to inspire oneself and others. *In business the word love equates precisely to a sense of caring, compassion, kindness, understanding, and commitment.* If you have ever been inspired by a person, you may recall that even though that person may have been demanding, he or she also had a deep, sincere interest in your well-being and demonstrated the caring and compassion that supported that commitment.

This critical attribute of Inspirational Leadership® appears throughout successful businesses and the arts. For example, as Lance Secretan reminds us in *The Spark, the Flame and the Torch,* in James Cameron's film *Avatar,* the Na'vi people from the planet Pandora greet each other with, "I see you." This acknowledges that they see the other person as being like themselves and in this sacred recognition, they understand that they are connected in some way, and that whatever they do to the other, they do unto themselves. Similarly, the Indian Sanskrit greeting "Namaste" means "The spirit in me respects the spirit in you."[95]

Being a caring person does not mean always doing what others may want or like. But in the end, your actions should inspire them because of your compassionate commitment to their well-being, as shown in my following personal example.

Some years ago, I hired a key executive for Catalytica. Ron (not his real name) was a bright young man with lots of energy and experience in our industry so I felt he could help us build Catalytica. Shortly after hiring Ron, I began to hear rumblings from customers that he was at times quite arrogant. Over a period of time I found out that he was an alcoholic. I was dismayed, but also determined to help him.

I confronted Ron and told him that Catalytica would pay for him to enroll in a program to help him deal with his personal challenge. However, I pointed out that should he ever be caught drinking alcoholic beverages again while working or come to work under the influence of alcohol, he would be fired immediately. He was pleased with Catalytica's and my personal commitment to him and agreed to undergo several weeks of treatment.

Ron returned to work and for a while all was well. However, two months after his return, he showed up at a customer's office blatantly intoxicated. I immediately, and much to my chagrin, fired Ron. I received an urgent telephone call from his wife to please reconsider. I refused, at which point she became quite angry with me.

Three years later I ran into Ron and his wife at a dinner. They asked to see me in private, at which time they both expressed their gratitude for my "tough love" in dealing with Ron. It forced them to face up to a critical issue, and even though they went through "living hell" for awhile, after receiving psychological counseling and extensive medical treatment Ron had now been "dry" for two years and had landed a successful job with another company. I was so pleased to see his recovery and success.

Ironically, love is the most difficult of the CASTLE Principles™ to define, yet arguably the most powerful attribute for inspiring people around you. Or, as Lance Secretan states so eloquently, "For all our bravado, and the legacy of learning about warrior leadership, we are now realizing that greatness and inspiration come from love, not war; they come from compassion and empathy, not from victory, violence, and domination. Our 'old-story' model of leadership is evolving quickly: the ruthless, ambitious, hard-charging A-type achiever is giving way to a 'New Story'—the caring, listening, mentoring leader who yearns to make the world a better place and to serve."[96]

Effectiveness

> *Efficiency is doing things right; effectiveness is doing the right things.*[97]
>
> —PETER DRUCKER

Effectiveness is the last of the CASTLE Principles and is actually the result of doing the first five principles well. And in fact, in a circular way of thinking, Effectiveness is both a cause and an effect. Inspirational Leaders are most effective when they have developed the skills to be Courageous, Authentic, Serving, Truthful, and Loving (or Caring, if you wish). When these attributes become a true part of our character, we cannot help but be personally inspired and we cannot help but to deeply inspire others to perform well beyond all expectations. This is being effective!

The famous architect, futurist, and philosopher, Buckminster Fuller, had a profound perspective on inspiration and the genius of creativity and innovation. He noted that, "Everyone is born a genius, but the process of living 'de-geniuses' them." Following up on Fuller's philosophy, Lance Secretan notes that there are several elements to living effectively and therefore to supporting the first five CASTLE Principles.[98]

- ❖ To be Effective, we must break old habits and restore our innate personal qualities.

- ❖ Pursuing the first Principle of Courage is simple, though not easy to do.

- ❖ We need to constantly look for rebirth and re-creation.

- ❖ If anything is unappealing, complicated, harmful, dangerous, destructive, or dishonest, it will ultimately fail. Negative energy requires forcing something that is unnatural—and nature always wins out in the long run. If it is graceful, elegant, caring, and honest, it will ultimately win because the very essence of nature is elegance and grace. Every successful scientific insight and theory into the workings of nature has always found surprising simplicity and elegance.

- ❖ Uninspiring tasks are difficult to achieve and more often than not, they fail.

- ❖ If a strategy or goal is an overt and purposeful personal affront to others, it will have negative consequences and in the end, fail. Respect the concept of "Oneness"—the interconnection with others—and in this recognition success will follow.[99]

In an analogy created by Buckminster Fuller, one can see that it only takes a single person to bring about incredible results that can change the world through Inspirational Leadership. Fuller reminds us that steering a large ocean liner requires moving the large rudder at the rear of the ship.

But how is this accomplished in practice? At the edge of the large rudder, there is a tiny device called a trim tab. It's a miniature rudder. Moving the trim tab just a little bit builds up a low pressure on one face of the large rudder relative to the other side and consequently pulls it around. This makes almost no effort at all.

To be an inspirational leader, you too can be a trim tab. You can inspire yourself and those around you. You can change the world.

CHAPTER 8

Power Performance Reviews

To what end, and to whose benefit, are our employees being asked to give of themselves? Have we committed ourselves to a purpose that is truly deserving of their initiative, imagination, and passion?[100]

—GARY HAMEL

KEY CONCEPTS

❖ Depending on company culture and the means of administration, performance reviews can be either a negative or positive tool in efforts to achieve fully-engaged, committed employees and a successful company.

❖ To add company value, appraisals should be conducted in a fair manner that accurately recognize the two-way function of the employee-supervisor team relationship and provide concrete information on how best to build that relationship and align the employee's goals with those of the company.

❖ A performance review should not focus on what the employee did *wrong*. It should be a celebration by the employee and supervisor of what worked for them, and it should determine how the employee and the supervisor, as a team, can do better in the subsequent year in view of what they have learned together. This means that constructive feedback from the employee to the supervisor is important and that this input should be graciously received and acted upon.

❖ A specific technique and format that has proven successful for the author in building several companies is provided.

Performance Review—Or Not?

Every January many of us are involved in an annual performance review, either giving or receiving one—or both. If you are a CEO, it is the time when you will likely look back over your company's performance for the year and ask, "How did we do? What should we be proud of? What have we, as a team, learned that can help us do even better in the future?" In your thoughtful reminiscence you might also ask, "What did each of our company team members do that is worthy of celebration and reward, and what have we learned that will help us support each other in future efforts towards individual, team, and corporate goals? In the spirit of Jim Collins, "How can we transition our company from good to great?"

It's performance review time! To many people in most companies this is a frightening experience, both for those receiving performance reviews and those giving them—especially if either one of the participants feels there is criticism that should be presented and discussed.

Performance reviews are a controversial subject. Some executives feel they are useless, contentious, and even deleterious. That need not be the case if conducted in an appropriate manner. More critically: without honest, well-designed reviews and constructive discussion, it is challenging—perhaps not even possible—to build a truly successful company for the long term.

The key word here is "successful." What is success, anyway? For me, *the best definition of success was formulated many years ago by motivational author and speaker, Earl Nightingale. **Success is the progressive realization of a worthy goal or ideal to which you are personally committed.*** This applies to people and companies alike. Therefore, if in an organization there are employees who do not understand and commit to the corporate goals and strategy, and subsequently cannot set their goals in a way that supports those of the company, how can either be successful?

At Catalytica, Inc. we developed a performance review system that was valuable to both employees and the company. It was not a fearful process, and it was an important contributor to our success as a company. I have refined this process over time, and currently we use it successfully at Chateau Mcely. Although the input form I present below applies especially to supervisors, managers, and executives, non-relevant points are easily eliminated where appropriate, so that much of the remaining content is directly adaptable to all employees.

Its prime purpose is to align all employee goals with those of the company, to identify effective means to further develop employees, and in achieving both of these objectives to create a fulfilling professional life for all employees and a successful enterprise.[101] Furthermore, the form is designed so that concerns over aspects of the employee's performance that did not work well during the year are inevitably raised by the employee and not the supervisor. Then, the approach is not to punish but to discover what has been learned and what can help the employee in going forward.

Last Year's Results; Next Year's Plan

Over the years we developed a very helpful form that is completed by the employee. Where necessary, the employee is given assistance from his or her supervisor in order to provide it to the supervisor at least one week before the review session. This input is discussed and modified as mutually considered necessary with the supervisor during or immediately after the review. The supervisor is responsible for *facilitating* the performance review. This means that he or she should be trained in effective communication skills—especially listening skills—to do so successfully. This is a very important requirement of the review process.

It requires considerable time and effort to complete this form for the first time, but in subsequent reviews it is much easier. Filling it out properly to the best of the employee's ability also requires that the company management be open and transparent with employees concerning relevant financial and other strategic data. The employee must clearly understand his or her specific expected role and contribution. Therefore, clarity of and commitment to the overall company strategy, goals, and tactics are very important.

Equally essential is that the employee and supervisor both understand and agree to the employee's *measurable* goals in contributing to the corporate strategy and achieving the annual plan.

Form Completed by Employee Prior to Performance Review[*]

1. List the following financial data.

	Last Year's Plan	Last Year's Actual Data	This Year's Plan
Sales			
Pre-Tax Profit			
EBITDA[†]			
Number of Employees (EOY)[‡]			
Sales Due to Employee's Team			

[*]Items in **bold print** are generally reserved for higher level managers and executives.
[†]EBITDA - Earnings before interest, taxes, depreciation, and amortization.
[‡]EOY - End of year.

2. List the top two to three significant events, both exciting and challenging, that happened during the year and had an impact on your performance.

3. If you could relive last year, what actions would you take differently?

4. What did you learn last year that you believe has future value to you and to the company?

5. What do you believe are the current external threats to our company and to our industry?

6. What is your role, if any, in helping our company to address these threats?

7. What new external and internal opportunities do you see for our company?

8. What are the one to three most significant issues or dilemmas you currently face within the context of your job?

9. **What do you understand are the essential elements of our current business strategy for the next year, and how do they apply to your position?**

10. **What are the two or three things that *must* happen to make our strategy work this year? How does this apply to your area of operation?**

11. What do you understand are the company goals for this year?

12. What are your team and personal corporate goals for this year?

13. How do you believe I could help you this year to achieve these goals?

14. **Who are our customers and what good news are we delivering to them?**

15. **Who are our competitors and what competitive advantage are we striving for?**

16. **What is the company doing, and what specifically are you doing, to help achieve this advantage?**

17. **As you review our company's strategic plan *for the next one to three years*, and you study the area for which you are respon-**

sible, what changes do you foresee in (a) our products and services, (b) our market scope, (c) the general size and profitability of our markets (increase or decrease.)

18. How will you spend your time this year in order to be consistent with your priorities?

19. What feedback do you want to give me so that I can help you become an even more successful employee? In particular, what did I do this past year that facilitated your job, and what did I do that made it more challenging for you.

20. What input can you give me to help me grow as an even more successful manager?

Providing answers to these twenty questions and having a constructive conversation between the two people involved in the performance review requires a corporate culture that is open and respectful of honest, compassionate input to both the employee and the supervisor or manager. They must see themselves and each other as important parts of their team. In a very real sense, they must see themselves as one. A company that develops such a culture has a significant competitive advantage, and is almost always a market leader.

Some might think that this approach requires too much time, is too transparent, and perhaps a bit too progressive. True, it does require a considerable amount of quality time. And yes, it is quite transparent and surely can be considered progressive when compared to the norm. But is your goal, or your company's goal, to be the norm? Furthermore, this technique has proven successful in my personal experience with a number of businesses I have been intimately involved in over the last three decades. While there is significant effort required by both employee and supervisor, the benefits far outweigh the time and effort required for this process.

Progressive Review Procedures

What we used in our organizations was considered quite progressive at its time and continues to be at the forefront of performance review thinking. However, there are more progressive approaches, and I would like to highlight one particular example because it proves the point I am making here that an honest, frank, and supportive performance review makes for a good company. Linden Lab's corporate culture and performance appraisal technique is described in a recent book by Jeff Hollender and Bill Breen.[102] The company was founded in 1998, has revenues exceeding $75 million, and employs well-established—one might even say "famous"—high-tech professionals from companies such as Apple, Microsoft, Electronic Arts, and Disney. As a measure of its performance, in 2008 the company was awarded an Emmy for its online virtual reality environment product called *Second Life*.[103] Much of their success is due to their corporate culture. They consider themselves a ***community*** and not a company, and they behave that way.

Why a community? Because they believe that to inspire people into a passionate and compassionate mode of action within the workplace so that they deliver the very best every day, the organization must behave as a community, and not as a typical corporate hierarchy. As a communal company they have demonstrated that profits fuel the drive to meet a higher purpose and all stakeholders are treated fairly.

Support for this approach comes from a recent ambitious global study by HR consulting firm Towers Perrin,[104] in which they surveyed 90,000 employees in large and medium-sized companies across eighteen countries.[105] They measured how committed people feel about their work. The results are cause for some deep thought. An incredible 81 percent of respondents said they were disengaged or disenchanted at work. But most interestingly, although Towers Perrin noted that quite often employees care a lot about their work and want to learn and grow, unfortunately many companies not only waste their people's talent and knowledge, but also actively discourage their employees from contributing more, even though most employees reported that they would like to do so. So how did Linden Lab break the bureaucratic hierarchy?

The management wanted to find ways to eliminate fear, which pervades many people in the workplace. Fear can make people worry about looking foolish in a meeting, or perhaps they have a fear of not living up to expectations, or maybe even the fear of losing their job. As discussed in chapter 5, fear constricts us and works against innovation and creativity. To minimize such fear, Linden Lab wanted to create a community-based culture that espoused virtues such as *happiness, caring, altruism, autonomy*, and *service*. Sound familiar?

Philip Rosedale, Linden's founder and CEO for several years, developed for employees a number of novel interactive techniques, one of which he calls the "Love Machine." It is an intranet web page that allows any of Linden's employees to send a quick message of appreciation to a colleague. They call these "Love Notes." They have more than three hundred employees and each day a similar number of Love Notes or peer-to-peer "pats-on-the-back" make their way through Linden's Intranet. They use these Love Notes in their performance review process, thereby allowing the entire **community** to have input. Every three months, employees pick the ten notes that they think best capture their contributions to the company over the prior quarter. Those notes are used in each employee's performance review.

When Rosedale was CEO, each quarter he sent out a questionnaire to every employee and asked three questions:

1. Do you want to keep me or find a new CEO?
2. Over the last three months, was I more effective, or less so at my job?
3. Why?

The voting was anonymous, so that employees felt free to be open and honest. Rosedale shared the results with the entire company and with the company's board of directors. His thinking is that you can argue with one person, but not with the crowd. He notes that "When every third person says 'You're too scattered,' it's the truth."

Companies do not have to be as progressive or avant-garde as Linden Lab, but evaluating employee performance in a way that is fair, productive, personally supportive, and focuses on the employee-supervisor interface, can bring powerful and positive results. In the end great enterprises see themselves and are seen by others as ONE company, ONE team and, in the best of circumstances—ONE person.

CHAPTER 9

Creating an
Innovative Environment

Most human beings are creative in some sphere of their lives ...
History shows that innovation almost always comes from unex-
pected quarters, often from individuals who appeared quite
ordinary to their friends and family. Sir Godfrey Hounsfield
inventor of the CAT scanner never earned a university degree.
Neither did Richard Branson, who got his start selling records
from the trunk of his car.[106]

—GARY HAMEL

KEY CONCEPTS

❖ The distinct elements and differences among creativity, discovery, invention, and innovation are important to understand in order to foster an innovative corporate culture.

❖ Entrepreneurs and Intrapreneurs: although easier to create in a smaller company, through top management leadership an innovative culture can be built into large firms as well.

❖ There are key elements, which when pursued and practiced diligently, help leadership create a long-term innovative culture.

❖ These elements encompass deep trust in executive leadership and an inspiring corporate "Dream," the success of which can make a positive difference in the world.

Creativity, Discovery, and Invention or Innovation?

ECONOMIST THEODORE LEVITT WAS FOND OF SAYING, *"Creativity is thinking up new things. Innovation is doing new things."* You might say that *creativity* is thinking of new ways to potentially solve a problem or address a need, and that *innovation is making it happen for the purpose of getting a desired return—financial, social, psychological, spiritual, or some combina-*

tion of the four. Someone who brings something new into existence has created it. This, I believe, is not innovation unless the person has managed to put it to a desirable use and receives an acceptable return.

The entire spectrum of innovation can be thought of as follows. In its earliest phase, innovation may, although not necessarily, start with a discovery. *Discovery is uncovering something that already exists but is unknown to all.* In 1953, James Watson and Francis Crick *discovered* the structure of DNA. The structure clearly already existed for billions of years, but was unknown to humanity until then. In 1947, William Shockley, John Bardeen, and Walter Brattain, working at Bell Labs, *invented* the transistor. Up until that time, the transistor and the transistor effect, which were responsible for a large percentage of the prosperity and global growth of the last century, did not exist. In other words, an inventor creates something that did not exist before, while a discovery is finding something which, up until that point in time, was completely unknown—but existed.

A discovery may move to the next step, which is invention, creating something novel that was previously unknown. The third and final step in the broad spectrum of innovation is bringing an invention to the marketplace and generating a return. Watson and Crick's discovery of the structure of DNA, while at the time seemingly just academic, fundamental science, ultimately led to numerous important inventions and innovations in molecular biology, for example, Tissue Plasminogen Activator (TPA), to name just one.

TPA was found to dissolve blood clots. Genentech, the first and one of the most successful genetic engineering firms, brought TPA through clinical trials to the marketplace, creating a major innovation and generating a large financial return for its shareholders. TPA created huge social returns by saving the lives of millions of cardiac arrest victims. My father was one of them. At seventy years of age, he "died" twice in a Dallas hospital emergency room, ultimately resuscitated and saved by an injection of TPA. He lived comfortably for another fifteen years.

Many inventors are successful at creating new products, but are unsuccessful as innovators because they fail to bring their invention to the marketplace and achieve customer satisfaction. More often than not, this is because they are passionately focused on just creating the invention and care less about a return, especially a financial return. Their intense need to create something that never existed before is often an intimate part of their very essence or "soul." In a way, they are like artistic purists who simply want to paint for creative satisfaction and care less if their works of art are appreciated by others and purchased, thereby providing them with a financial return.

Another example may be helpful. In December of 1979 Steve Jobs paid a visit to Xerox's Palo Alto Research Center (PARC) in Palo Alto, California, where he was shown the mouse-driven Alto computer developed at PARC. It was the first truly functioning personal computer; however, it was not a commercial device and was used exclusively by engineers and scientists within the PARC laboratories. Furthermore, the mouse-driven point-and-click technology, which was invented at PARC, was also unknown in the marketplace. Jobs was so impressed with this "insanely great" idea that he "borrowed" it and built the mouse system into Apple's Lisa and Macintosh computers. The latter became an enormous commercial success, primarily because of the point-and-click technology. The designer at PARC who built the Alto Computer was the *inventor*; but Jobs, who successfully introduced PARC's computer mouse technology to the marketplace, was the *innovator*. Apple's innovation was felt in literally every computer developed after that; all incorporated point-and-click technology.

Entrepreneur or Intrapreneur?

An innovative environment is often generated and fostered in small companies by an *entrepreneur—a passionate change-maker, who brings together talent, capital, and novel ideas to create or address a need in the marketplace for the sake of making a positive difference and generating a return.* That's exactly what Steve Jobs and Steve Wozniak did for Apple in 1976 with the development of the Apple I, their first commercial computer. In larger firms, an innovative environment may be the result of efforts of what Gifford Pinchot III has called an "intrapreneur."[107]

An intrapreneur is generally thought of as a person within a large corporation who takes direct responsibility for turning an idea into a profitable finished product through assertive risk-taking and innovation. Both entrepreneur and intrapreneur are risk takers, driven by an idea that they passionately believe will not only make a positive difference, but will also bring a return to their stakeholders and perhaps much more.

Building an intrapreneurship culture into a large company is a challenge, but it can be done. Over the last couple of decades, the intrapreneurial concept of "skunk works," which grew out of Lockheed Martin's successful experience in developing high-performance aircrafts, has permeated the business literature and in some cases has won the day, often despite the challenges of a large corporate culture. In this mode of action, a team is given a high level of autonomy and is not hampered by normal corporate bureaucracy. Some examples of success include 3M's Post-It Notes, Audi's Quattro, IBM's first PC, Ford's Mustang, and Toyota's Prius.

Although both entrepreneurs and intrapreneurs are generally innately driven, becoming the "engines" of innovation, there are some characteristics of these unique people that can be built into any company and will foster innovative thought-processes, behavior, and goals—even when they do not spring from one driven individual. These characteristics can be learned and successfully put into practice in both small and large companies.

Characteristics of an Innovative Environment

Let's summarize those key characteristics, which if pursued and practiced diligently, can create a lasting innovative environment in the workplace.

Trust, the single most reliable predictor of employee satisfaction and productivity is necessary to create an innovative environment. Trust must percolate through the entire fabric of the company. In chapter 7 we discussed the elements necessary for lasting trust as one of the fundamental assets of an Inspirational Leader. They are worth repeating.

❖ The top leadership must excite all of the stakeholders with their vision for the company.

❖ Employees must understand, and to an appropriate degree, participate in developing the company's strategy—at least that part which applies to successful accomplishment of their efforts towards agreed upon goals.

❖ Employees must intimately understand how their role can contribute to achieving the company's goals.

❖ Top leadership must share with employees the company's progress, and how their individual teams are doing relative to their team goals as well as toward the company goals; and the leadership must do so with impeccable candor.

Leaders must create a vision and mission—a "Dream"—that begs for innovation, and they must continuously show their personal commitment to this "Dream," and to the innovation process.

Dreams are powerful motivators and have a way of inspiring employees to achieve extraordinary goals. Dreams also evaporate differences among people so that everyone contributes to the success. During World War II, Republicans and Democrats alike worked side-by-side to achieve a challenging victory in the name of freedom. It took extraordinary leadership to move the entire country in this direction, but once aligned, the power of the American effort was extraordinary.

The company's energies must be focused on a "Dream" that will make a positive difference in the world.

As discussed throughout this book, everyone is born with a specific skill or set of skills—something that differentiates them from those around them and which, when personally discovered, can generate a deep desire to apply that skill to something that can make a significant positive difference in this world. And when we link our skills with a specific need in the world, passion is generated that sometimes not only can make a difference, but can change the world significantly for the better. Famous examples of people who experienced this transition and journey include Albert Einstein, Marie Curie, Leonardo da Vinci, Mahatma Gandhi, and numerous lesser-known, yet successful men and women, some of whom you may have met throughout your life.

Innovation must be required by and connected to corporate strategy.

If the company *Dream* is big enough to excite employees and the leadership, it is likely to require discovery or invention of non-obvious solutions to certain goals. It will "beg" for innovation. At Apple computer it was Steve Jobs' obsession with "insanely great" products that motivated employees to solve challenging problems, either in-house or with the help of outside expertise. Apple didn't care where the ideas came from. They often put together well-known disparate pieces of information in a creative way to assemble and launch an innovation. They were driven to create the best possible product and get it into the marketplace by innovations that allowed them to have a final product that was superb in function, but reasonable in manufacturing cost. That's why Apple's iPhone, though capturing a small percentage of the global cell-phone market, has consistently had the highest absolute level of profit among all cell-phone companies, worldwide.

Employees should have a high level of autonomy in doing their job.

Did you ever work for someone who said to you, "This is a problem we need to solve. We need a solution in six months. I know you have the expertise and capabilities to address this problem. Do you think you can deliver an acceptable solution?" You answered, "Yes," and then, except for an occasional brief update, you were left completely on your own to find the solution. Yes, you had access to others if you chose to pursue their guidance, but basically, you decided the path to take. Do you recall the sense of trust, confidence, personal passion, and excitement that you felt? It is empowering beyond what many managers comprehend. And it is not only empowering, but more often than not, it delivers results because the personal passion created by this approach stimulates the creative thought process.

The company culture must tolerate smart "mistakes" and learn from them.

Remember that Teflon, the microwave oven, penicillin, Post-It Notes, Velcro, and Viagra, among many other inventions and discoveries, were all "mistakes."

- ❖ In April of 1938, Dr. Roy Plunckett at DuPont was working with a new refrigerant gas, tetrafluoroethylene, called Freon®. A metal cylinder of tetrafluoroethylene did not seem to have any gas in it, although it was known by Dr. Plunkett to be a full cylinder. Being curious, he asked his lab technician to saw the cylinder in half. Plunkett's curiosity paid off. When the technician opened the cylinder, he found that the gas, catalyzed by metallic particles inside the cylinder, had polymerized to a white waxy material. Teflon® had been discovered.

- ❖ Dr. Percy Spencer, an engineer at Raytheon Corporation was experimenting in 1946 with a newly designed vacuum tube called a magnetron when he found that a candy bar in his pocket melted when he activated the tube. Curious as to what was happening, Percy started up the magnetron tube again, this time placing kernels of corn next to it. The corn popped—the microwave heating oven was invented.

◆ In 1928 bacteriologist Alexander Fleming unexpectedly found a mold had contaminated one of his experiments. Frustrated by the results, he decided to pursue what caused the contamination. In the course of his experiments and to his amazement, he found the mold to have powerful antibacterial properties. He named the active agent "penicillin." As the first major antibiotic, it has since saved millions of lives.

❖ Arthur Fry working in 1974 at 3M remembered that a "useless" glue had been invented by his colleague, Spencer Silver. The glue was weak, thus not a very good adhesive. Yet it was reusable and easily removed from paper without leaving a mark. Silver had tried unsuccessfully to think of a use for the glue. It was Fry who just happened to decided to use it to stick papers in his Bible to mark the Sunday readings. The Post-it Notes were born, a huge international success for 3M.

❖ For millennia, people have hiked through fields and picked up cockleburs on their clothing—a real nuisance. In 1948 George de Mestral, a Swiss engineer experiencing the same problem, wondered what caused these things to stick to his clothing. He examined the cockleburs under a microscope and noticed thin strands of *hooks* that caught to the *loops* of threads on his socks. A tenacious inventor, over the next eight years de Mestral experimented intensely and finally found a means to create loops on one surface and hooks on another, both from polymeric materials. This discovery provided the basis for the invention that we today recognize as VELCRO®.

❖ In 1994 my company Catalytica Pharmaceuticals was working with Pfizer Pharmaceuticals, one of our major investors, when we heard the following story from Pfizer employees. Nicholas Terrett and his colleague Peter Ellis were testing a new drug candidate called Sildenafil as a heart drug. Because of its molecular structure and prior experience with similar structures, they were confident that there was an excellent possibility the drug would increase blood flow to the heart. It failed to do so, but instead provided an enormous increase in blood flow to the penis in male patients. It was later found that the drug acts by enhancing the smooth muscle relaxant effects of nitric oxide, a chemical stimulator—neurotransmitter—

that is normally released in response to sexual stimulation. The smooth muscle relaxation allows increased blood flow to the per is leading to a long-lasting, rigid erection. Sildenafil citrate became the active ingredient of the widely popular drugs Viagra, Revatio, and various other trade name products used to treat erectile dysfunction. Our Pfizer colleagues told us a number of the male participants refused to return any of their Sildenafil that was unused in the clinical trials!

Mistakes? What mistakes?

There should be consistent, two-way communication with employees on company progress towards its goals.

Depending on company size, one of the best ways to do this with some regularity is to have company or departmental meetings once each month, and as part of that meeting to ask one team to present a 15–20-minute summary of their progress. When at all possible the CEO should be present, or at a minimum, one or more of the highest level executives in the company. At these meetings solid progress should be celebrated in some manner—if even just applause—and setbacks should be recognized as a natural consequence of the creative learning process—recall my comments above concerning mistakes! It may well be that someone from another team has an idea that could lead to a solution to the challenge at hand, or perhaps to a different and completely unanticipated innovation.

Employees should understand their financial limit, although success is not always about money.

There is no such thing as unlimited funds. Budgets are necessary to be good stewards of your almost surely limited financial resources. When this understanding is built into the company culture, you will find that if a team is committed to success, when it knows that the budgeted funding is depleted yet feels a solution is truly around the corner, the team will either convince management to eke out a small amount of continued funding or do the work on its own time to achieve success.

Recently at Chateau Mcely, Mirek, our maintenance manager asked to buy a new John Deere tractor to replace our older model. Due to budget constraints, he was told by our managing director that we could not afford one this year. On his own, Mirek approached the John Deere management and told them that we would highlight and endorse our use of their equipment if they would take back our old tractor on a trade-in and give us the latest version—for no additional expense. Because the John Deere management highly regards Chateau Mcely's brand within the Czech Republic, they agreed!

Success is not necessarily connected to available funds. At the beginning of the last century the brilliant astronomer, physicist, and inventor, Samuel Pierpont Langley, was intensely experimenting with "heavier-than-air" machines trying to invent the first engine-powered aircraft to carry a passenger. Langley was born into a wealthy family and was well connected to some of the most powerful people in the United States. He had immense funds from the U.S. government to make his invention succeed. But two brothers who owned a bicycle shop in Dayton, Ohio, had a similar dream.

Orville and Wilbur Wright were of modest means and barely had a high-school education, but their fundamental essence—what they were really good at—was creative mechanics, hence the bicycle shop. They also had a dream to create the first powered passenger aircraft. On December 17, 1903, just south of Kitty Hawk, North Carolina, they succeeded. Two years later they built the first practical fixed-wing airplane. The brothers' fundamental breakthrough was their patented invention of a three-axis-control system which enabled the pilot to steer the aircraft effectively and safely maintain its equilibrium in takeoff, flight, and landing. Upon learning of the Wright bothers' success, a devastated Samuel Pierpont Langley immediately gave up his research. It's not always about the money.

Innovation throughout the company should be rewarded.

One of the biggest rewards for people working on a successful project that truly makes this a better world is simply that—the fact that they made the world a better place in which to live. However, a company should not stop there. A fair and effective psychological and financial reward system should be designed to fit the company's culture. This could include various components of the following:

❖ Private recognition by the CEO or by an appropriate high-level executive. At Catalytica, depending on the importance of the innovation, I would provide a hand-written note of thanks and an all-expense paid trip to a first-class resort for our employee and his or her significant other. This was meant to say "thank you" to both the employee and his partner for their support and for working diligently to help us succeed.

Public recognition by the CEO in a company meeting, or by some other highly visible mechanism.

❖ On the financial side, care must always be taken to be sure that all individuals as well as the team are rewarded for accomplishments. This usually requires careful input from key executives, the team leader, and perhaps certain team members. The total financial "pot" allocated for the accomplishment, whether it is stock options and/or bonuses, should be carefully distributed to recognize the achievement. This is not an easy task and it is highly subjective, so the more input the decision maker gets, the easier the task.

In the long run the process should recognize corporate, team, and individual contributions to the accomplishments. While early on in an individual's career the level of financial recognition may be important to manage his or her standard of living, with time it increasingly becomes a measure of the individual's or team's success and a direct indicator of management's positive feedback that accrues with this success. From that point of view, the reward is both financially and psychologically important to the recipient.

These elements, taken together, can not only be effective in recognizing innovation, but, equally important, they can help build a culture in which creative innovation is inculcated and stimulated. Very often these innovations would never have seen the light of day had the company leadership not been committed to these elements. It was our commitment to these nine elements of innovation that resulted in Catalytica's several hundred patents and a powerful competitive advantage in the marketplace.

As Edward de Bono has often said in his many books on the creative process, *"Creative thinking is not a talent; it is a skill that can be learned. It empowers people by adding strength to their natural abilities which improves teamwork, productivity and where appropriate, profits."* And in terms of *Cosmic Consciousness* and our universal connectedness, a commitment to these elements to build an innovative company culture not only can create a more successful company, but also helps build more fulfilled people and a better world in which to live.

CHAPTER 10

Conscious Capitalism: Preventing Economic Chaos

Today we find ourselves in a paradoxical situation. We enjoy all the achievements of modern civilization that have made our physical existence on earth easier in so many important ways. Yet we do not know exactly ourselves, where to turn ... There appear to be no integrating forces, no unified meaning, no true inner understanding of phenomena in our experience of the world. ... The abyss between the rational and the spiritual, the external and the internal, the objective and the subjective, the technical and the moral, the universal and the unique constantly grows deeper.[108]

—VACLAV HAVEL

KEY CONCEPTS

- ◆ Several global threats are key challenges to human sustainability via economic and social collapse.

- ◆ Addressing just one of them—Non-transparent Political and Corporate Governance—can help significantly to mitigate all global threats to human sustainability.

- ◆ Government can provide social, economic, and political incentives to address these critical challenges, but it is business which has evolved to the most powerful eco-technological force on the planet, and therefore must take responsibility for "the whole" and provide long-term viable solutions.

- ◆ In doing so, business will play the leading role in providing a just and sustainable future for humanity, and as a result enhance its own ultimate performance and long-term viability.

- ◆ The only viable strategy is to transition to **Conscious Capitalism**, in which conventional Motivational Leaders become or are replaced by **Conscious Leaders**.

- ◆ The power of this higher level of **Conscious Leadership** to serve all stakeholders, often called **Inspired Leadership** or **Inspirational Leadership**®, is beyond anything we have ever experienced with conventional leadership models.

Global Threats

THE WORLD HAS CHANGED. And as the late Vaclav Havel, the first president of the Czech Republic, notes in his prescient quote at the opening of this chapter, we stand at a critical tipping point in the history of the human race. Not long ago, for better or for worse, the world moved to a single global economy, a natural extension of our capitalist's creed. The pessimists among us would say "greed." This decision brought opportunities for many, but it also created the most critical challenges in human history For me, the most challenging global threats are:

Non-Transparent Political and Corporate Governance

Energy-Climate Insecurity

Nuclear Proliferation, Terrorism, and War

Cyber-terrorism

Global Pollution

Overpopulation

All either directly or indirectly promote poverty, civil unrest, and environmental unsustainability.

Some might disagree with my characterization of these challenges as *the* major threats to humanity, and especially the first one. But think for just a moment about the evolution of global power during the last millennium. For centuries, organized religion ruled much of the world. With time that power was overtaken by government, and then, beginning with the Industrial Revolution in the 18th century, business slowly but assuredly became *the* dominant global power. In many developed countries corporations heavily influence and often control government actions and decisions. It was precisely this power, focused in a negative direction and complemented by cooperative government support , that was responsible for the intense global financial challenges that became apparent beginning in 2008.

Business Is the Most Powerful Social Force

This means that if business, as the most powerful economic, technological, and societal force on the planet, does not lead the way to addressing our global challenges, it is unlikely that anyone or any institution will—or could—do so effectively. Although far from a universally accepted conclusior, this responsibility of business for "the whole" is not incompatible with a fair return to *all* stakeholders—people, planet, and profit—the so-called "Triple Bottom Line." In fact, if not addressed by business, these challenges will likely lead to civil unrest and even, under the best of circumstances, to significantly diminished business productivity.[109]

There are more than enough books that predict social upheaval, economic collapse,[110] and the unsustainability of life as we know it.[111] However, proof that corporations can move us in the right direction is demonstrated by the success of companies such as Patagonia, Whole Foods, UPS, Starbucks, The Body Shop, Medtronics, Google, Herman Miller, Vestas, and others. But as we progress into the twenty-first century, much, much more will be required.

For the human race to continue to thrive and proceed along a path of productive evolution of body, mind and consciousness, and to continue developing the social structure that supports this evolution, I believe that the world must transition to what has been called *Conscious Capitalism*.[112] I have touched on some of the central aspects of Conscious Capitalism in chapters 2 and 3 where I outlined how to unleash the power of purpose and passion. *Conscious Capitalism refers to the concept that profit and prosperity can and must embrace social justice and respect for our environment.*[113]

Perhaps to the surprise of many, particularly those entangled in old leadership models, *Conscious Capitalism almost always leads to a more successful enterprise regardless of the evaluation metric.* Most importantly, it is Conscious Capitalism that can provide a means for humanity to make a quantum jump to the "Next Paradigm" that increasing numbers of visionaries predict as the desired destination from the precarious cusp on which civilization currently teeters.

Transition to Conscious Capitalism

Conscious businesses are built on three core principles.[114] *First, a conscious business always seeks a higher purpose*, which need not be incompatible with profit, and more often than not, leads to profit maximization. It doesn't matter whether it is a beer company or a biotech firm, conscious commerce can be a practical and realistic goal. Whole Foods, led by cofounder and co-CEO John P. Mackey, is a purveyor of healthy natural products and one of the world's most socially conscious companies. It is also one of the most successful supermarkets.

Second, Conscious Businesses deliver value to ALL stakeholders by align-ing with their interests; this encompasses customers, employees, partners, investors, suppliers, community, and the planet. Patagonia, led by founder Yvon Chouinard, and a major supplier of outdoor and hiking clothing, does exactly this and yet continues to outperform its competitors.

And third, and most importantly, Conscious Businesses are led by Con-scious Leaders who focus on the company's deeper purpose and on delivering value to all stakeholders by finding creative, profitable means to harmonize and mesh their interests. Bill George, recently retired CEO of Medtronics and Professor at the Business School of Harvard University, has been called the "Model of Twenty-first Century Leadership" for his commitment to all stakeholders. Conscious Capitalism is not just a theory. These examples poignantly demonstrate that it works well with Inspirational Leaders at the helm.

Therefore, the central aspect of business and commerce that must be addressed to solve the critical issues we face as a global humanity is leadership. Since Adam Smith's treatise on *The Wealth of Nations,* written in 1776 at the inception of the Industrial Revolution, we have primarily taught and practiced two leadership styles. As we saw in chapter 7, for the longest time it was *Leadership via Fear and Threat.* During the 1960s most of the developed world began to "advance" to *Leadership by Reward,* that is, leadership by the "carrot and stick" model. However, even this form of leadership is ego-based and is driven primarily by the leader's personal needs and desires.[115] Such a leader is generally chosen based on past per-formance and he or she directs the organization to be coherent, cohesive, and effective. Because this form of leadership emanates from the ego, it is primarily driven by personal ambition, determination, goal attainment, and sometimes aggressiveness, and arrogance.

In broad terms, leadership can be seen to have evolved from *Hierarchal* (boss-employee relationships driven by the ego and the need for power)—developed at the inception of the Industrial Revolution—to *Motivational* (create an environment with psychological and financial perquisites and rewards driven by the employees perceived and apparent need for per-sonal advancement and goal achievement)—developed in the 1960s—to *Conscious* or *Inspirational* (inspire the leader who inspires employees, driven by a deep-seated need to create a profitable venture by helping to change the world for the better)—developed over the last decade. I believe that this evolution of leadership has occurred not only because we have evolved physically over the millennia, but, more importantly, because much of humanity has also evolved in its level of conciousness.[116]

During the past, there has always been a smattering of individuals with higher levels of consciousness, even gurus and saints. However, slowly but surely over the last several hundred years there has been an increase in the average level of consciousness. This can be seen in greater levels of personnel and social responsibility and a rapidly rising concern and commitment to address global threats. One need only briefly peruse the internet to see the large and growing number of socially responsible enterprises and organizations that have sprung up in the last two decades.

Inspired Leadership Is the Way[117]

In Motivational Leadership, the leader does something to others. For example, he or she seeks to **direct**—even **push**—employees towards the leader's agenda and his or her view of the appropriate objectives. This leadership style has served companies and governments reasonably well for the last half century, but it will not succeed in addressing the six global challenges listed at the beginning of this chapter. Why? Worldwide environmental consciousness is rapidly growing; public distrust of corporations with its current base of leadership is at an all-time high; many employees and customers are disengaged from the companies they work for or buy from, respectively; suppliers feel alienated and squeezed on price; and, often communities organize to keep businesses out of their proximity.

As discussed in chapter 4, a recent major study by world-renowned strategist Gary Hamel concludes that 80 percent of employees are disengaged and unsatisfied with their job.[118] We desperately need a new kind of leadership, one that speaks to all of the stakeholders and is focused on the Triple Bottom Line. Such an approach has been developed by a number of forward-looking thinkers.[119] It is called Conscious Leadership, Inspired Leadership, or Inspirational Leadership® and is described in great detail in chapter 7.[120] The consciousness of a rapidly increasing fraction of humanity is ready for this kind of leadership. It yearns for it. We will need it to survive!

Inspired Leadership is a serving relationship with others that inspires them to grow and reach their innate human potential, and in doing so they not only exhibit outstanding performance and thereby contribute much more to their company, but they also make the world a better place. Inspired Leadership is not a model or a formula or a system or a process. Instead of ***doing*** something to someone, Inspired Leadership is a way of ***being*** and it comes from within, from your very spirit, your soul, your consciousness, or whatever you wish to call the fundamental essence within each human being.

You can choose to be this way, you don't have to be promoted or anointed. *Its two central hallmarks are awareness of your true self within and the world around you, and responsibility for "the whole."* It is also the only form of leadership that has been shown over and over again to result in lasting fulfillment and true personal and professional balance. Inspired Leadership is very powerful and it inspires greatness from one person to others. Success in ego-based Motivational Leadership focuses on power, profit, and market dominance. You might ask yourself, "Who has been more successful in their life journey and made a greater impact on humanity, Motivational Leaders such as former Chrysler CEO, Lee Iacocca, former General Electric CEO Jack Welch, or Inspired Leaders such as Medtronic's past CEO Bill George, Whole Foods Co-CEO John P. Mackey, or former South African President Nelson Mandela?"

It's Not the Economy, Stupid—It's the Need for Inspiration

> *When you are inspired by some great purpose, some extra-ordinary project, all your thoughts break their bonds; your mind transcends limitations, your consciousness expands in every direction, and you find yourself in a new great wonderful world. Dormant forces, faculties and talents become alive, and you discover yourself to be a greater person than you ever dreamed yourself to be.*[121]
>
> —PATANJALI, author of the *Yoga Sutras*, 150 B.C.

Conscious or inspired leaders take full responsibility for all relationships, from employees, family, and friends to the well-being of the planet and our species. Being conscious means being fully aware, totally engaged and personally responsible for the impact you have on the world, as well as the impact the world has on you. So the very first thing an inspired leader does is to gain deep insight into his or her own life and the inspiring role that he or she can play in both the personal and business arenas, and the responsibility that comes with the inspiration of others.

How to do this has been discussed in detail in chapters 2, 3, and 4. The essence of it all is to understand your true purpose in life. What sets you apart from others around you that would allow you to contribute to the greater good? This *knowledge of purpose,* when connected with a need in this world, always leads to *passion* for action, which ignites energy and *inspiration* that generates *creativity,* which in turn results in *innovation,* historically the single factor that has created the largest number of jobs. Isn't that what makes companies "great" and the world a better place? To be sure, inspired leadership is not just a charitable undertaking. Pursued and practiced with integrity, it results in substantial returns to all stakeholders. It builds better, longer-lasting institutions that are a source of fulfillment for the "whole."

By a commitment to this process of introspection and change, it is possible to understand the role that you can play in transforming the organization you lead—or work within—into one that truly inspires you and those around you. The core force of this transformation process is *inspiration,* fueled by compassion and caring for others. History teaches us that it is inspiration that gets things done, creates ideas, grows people—it can change the world.

OneDream™

Once you understand your personal sense of purpose in the business world, and your passion is ignited, it is a natural next step to create what Lance Secretan calls *OneDream™,* the vision and mission that underpins your organization.[122] It is this *OneDream* that attracts and motivates others to your path, and you will get things done through others and at the same time this will help them to grow well beyond their expectations and they will feel incredibly fulfilled and balanced, both personally and professionally.

The power of OneDream can be seen in the example of U.S. President John F. Kennedy's commitment for the U.S. to go to the moon as discussed in chapter 5. His dream was created on October 4, 1957, when the Soviets launched Sputnik 1, the first earth-orbiting artificial satellite. Feuding Republicans and Democrats alike stood behind Kennedy. Dreams are like that—they transcend differences and disagreements—they join people at a higher level of consciousness, engage them in a higher purpose—as ONE![123] Dreams have the power to change the world, and have done so, many times before.

It's All about Trust

*Inspired Leaders are intimately aware of the single most reliable predictor of employee productivity and satisfaction—**TRUST**!* And as discussed in detail in chapters 7 and 9, they understand the means to foster and cultivate trust in their organization.

Examples of recent Inspired Leaders include Nelson Mandela, Martin Luther King, Bill George (former CEO of Medtronics—sales of $16 billion/year), Ray Anderson (founder of Interface, Inc.—sales of $1 billion/year), Robert Swanson (founder of Genentech—$10 billion/year), and Yvon Chouinard (founder of Patagonia, Inc.—$320 million/year). Take the example of Ray Anderson, founder and recently retired CEO of the world's largest manufacturer of modular carpets. Carpet manufacturing is notorious for pollution. Since 1995, under Anderson's leadership and supported by employees as part of their *OneDream*, Interface has reduced its waste by one-third and is on target to reach its goal of making the company environmentally sustainable by 2020. Anderson's company is consistently the most profitable carpet company in the developed world, proof that the Triple Bottom Line—People, Planet, Profit—works!

Can We Do It?

The big question is, "At a time that is arguably the most critical tipping point in the history of mankind, will we slip into economic, environmental, and social chaos, or can we make the transition to a higher state of consciousness in the way we do business?" I believe that we can, perhaps not without a few false starts and minor "catastrophes," but the global human spirit will eventually triumph. I am sure of it. History has often gifted us with the right leaders at the right time to catalyze a necessary quantum change in human consciousness—Thomas Jefferson, Abraham Lincoln, Franklin Delano Roosevelt, Winston Churchill, Mahatma Gandhi, Vaclav Havel, and Nelson Mandela, to name a few. But I think this time things are different.

If we are to create a sustainable future for us, for our children, and for all our descendants thereafter, it will require more than a "chosen few" to make the transition. It will require broad participation in Inspired Leadership in much of what we do—an immediate commitment by you, by me, and many more like us. ***Whether you are a housewife, a merchant, a politician, or a CEO, you must show your courage and commitment to our future and support only those institutions, people, products, and services that***

will help create a sustainable future for our children. If you take just a brief moment and look deep into your soul, your conscious being, you will find that there really is no other choice. As Hillel the Elder, a wise Rabbi who lived during the time of Christ said so poignantly, "If not you ... who? If not here ... where? If not now ... when?"[124]

Appendix A

My 2005 Life Plan[125]

(Prepared January 3, 2005)

My Plan for the Spheres of Personal and Professional Growth

Social Relationships Sphere

1. I support my family & friends

I listen to understand and I am not judgmental in my remarks. I work diligently to provide the emotional and financial support that I believe is required by my family. I spend quality time with them to nurture our respective spirits.

2. I pursue and develop friendships.

I work at developing friendships and especially at building on my current ones. I do this by trying new things and through visiting, remembering, and being there.

Spiritual Sphere

3 I practice honesty and integrity.

I am honest with myself and with others in all my actions. I work diligently at erasing earlier "mind tapes" that do not fit my values. I seek to understand without prejudging. Honest and earnest inquiry is my constant companion.

4 I practice and build my spirituality.

I spend time every day in meditation for gratitude, understanding, and fortitude. It is at least as important to me to foster my spiritual and emotional growth and to continuously raise my level of consciousness, as it is to enhance my physical well-being. I understand that with everything that I learn, the Universe is incredibly beautiful, remarkable, and simultaneously complex and simple. I believe it was initiated and is governed by the laws of the ***First Force***.[126]

5. **I give back to humanity through personal commitment of time and financial support.**

   Through my talents in entrepreneurship, communication, leadership, and entertainment, I contribute financially and by dedication of personal time to those needs of humanity that I feel are important and will raise the consciousness of the Universe.

6. **I seek fun and the positive in all that I do.**

   I look at the positive side in all situations without dispensing with reality and without violating my basic principles. I always remember that it takes as much effort—perhaps more—to live a miserable life as it does a great one.

Professional Sphere

7. **I build profitable entrepreneurial enterprises that contribute to society.**

   I channel my professional energies into building and/or fostering the growth of profitable entrepreneurial enterprises that are comprised of a culture that enables the spiritual, personal, and professional growth and development of the participants. These enterprises market products and/or services that help continually advance the quality of life of humanity.

Financial Sphere

8. **I increase our family wealth as necessary to accomplish our goals.**

   I increase our family wealth as a means to accomplish our goals, but not for aberrant and excessive collection of material things and ego satisfaction.

Health Sphere

9. **I stay healthy and vital.**

   I exercise daily to maintain a healthy body and mind. I continuously envision myself as a very healthy individual and seek new ways to build my spiritual, emotional, and physical vitality.

Knowledge Sphere

10. I continuously build my conscious self through leadership and learning.

I build on and leverage my strengths (leadership, vision, optimism, technical knowledge, communication, entertainment experience, and high-energy level), and I address areas in which I seek improvement and growth (patience, analysis, non-judgment, and personal discipline). I enhance my being through courses, reading, travel, self-learning, reflection, team building, and asking for feedback from family and friends. I integrate this feedback and learning into building and honing my persona, my mind, and my psyche.

11. I use time management to balance my life within the Six Spheres of Universal Growth.

I review daily how I spend my time and I adjust my actions, when necessary, to be in accord with proper balance among my values and goals.

My Goals and Actions

Social Sphere Relationships:

Family and friends are a critical part of my life. I work to grow these relationships. I develop other friendships outside the family.

My Goals

I will continue to build on my relationship with Inez as measured by her feedback.

I will continue to build on my relationship with Polly and Doreen—as measured by their feedback.

I will develop a closer contact with my immediate family.

I will seek new friends in Prague.

My Actions

I spend at least two to three quality hours with Inez every day.

I speak with Mom at least once per week and visit her in the United States twice per year.

I speak with or e-mail Polly and Doreen at least twice per month. I visit with them in the United States twice per year.

I will send Chuck, Tom, Lisa, Camille, Sal, Grace, Tina, Terry, and Donna a copy of my recent CD.

I control my emotions and listen to understand—without judgment—until I have the facts.

I assume the positive and banish negative thoughts about people and things.

I will socialize with at least one friend per month in Prague.

Spiritual:

I want to be at peace and spiritually connected with the *First Force,* my family and friends, humanity, and the Universe by having truly lived by my values and by understanding and accepting people for who they are. On my deathbed, I want to feel pleased with my life and welcome the "Next Step."

My Goals

Through daily meditation, I will increase my level of consciousness by December 31, as measured by Inez's input.

Before December 31, I will have at least one experience of a genuine sense of quiet and peace not unlike that when I climbed Mt. Kilimanjaro via the ice glacier.

I will give back to humanity through personal time and financial contribution, particularly helping economically and emotionally disadvantaged children, who I feel are an important part of our future.

My Actions

Meditate for twenty minutes every morning and evening.

Read one book per month on spiritualism and/or consciousness.

By December 31, I will sell one thousand of my CDs to help disadvantaged children.

Professional Sphere:

I build and/or foster the growth of profitable enterprises that contribute value to society. I support the concept of these enterprises by working to become a recognized author, teacher, and communicator who provides a valued perspective on the confluence of science, technology, the arts, and the environment with humanity.

My Goals

Within three years, I will help build Chateau Mcely into an international successful retreat and spa, and within a five-year time frame I will create a program to bring leading thinkers—"global change-makers"—to the Czech Republic and to Chateau Mcely to discuss implementable solutions to challenging social issues such as energy security, climate change, and the need for more conscious leadership in business.

I will initiate establishing myself as a competent writer.

I seek to help entrepreneurial companies.

I will launch our Leadership Project in Chateau Mcely.

My Actions

Complete the renovation of Chateau Mcely by September 30.

Recruit and train an effective core management team by March 1, 2005; lead team building and training exercises monthly—March through December.

Create an international marketing strategy by April 30, 2005.

Establish a reliable mechanism to financially manage Chateau Mcely by April 30, 2005.

By December 31, 2005, explore three or four mechanisms to create and brand a seminar program on Inspired Leadership at Chateau Mcely.

Chateau Mcely will be profitable by 2008.

Business opening: soft opening—May 1, 2006; formal opening—September 1, 2006.

Publish a monthly column by April 30.

Write three articles this year for the World Business Academy.

By April 30, launch our website for Chateau Mcely.

By April 15, complete a business plan for our Leadership project.

Support the World Business Academy for up to five hours per week.

Financial Sphere:

I will grow my wealth as a means to accomplish my goals, but not for aberrant and excessive collection of material things for ego satisfaction.

My Goals

Assure that our wealth is increasing by at least 10 percent per year by December 31.

I will have a continuously increasing net worth of X before age sixty-five with at least Y in readily liquid assets.

My Actions

Think three times before spending money for extras, preferably over a period of twenty-four hours.

By May 1, buy a new flat in Prague 1 and decide on the sale of Prague 6 flat.

By May 31, identify the means to achieve our overall financial goal.

Do a financial overview of all of our assets every quarter.

By March 31, develop a financial plan and tracking system for Chateau Mcely.

Physical & Mental Health Sphere:

I will exercise in some way every day of my life with the intent of staying physically and mentally healthy and maintaining a low morbidity rate until my "Last Moment."

My Goals

By exercising, by cutting down on desserts, carbohydrates, and alcohol, and by drinking more water, I will weigh 210 pounds by December 31.

My Actions

Go to bed by 11:00 p.m. and rise at 5:00 a.m.

Lift weights three days per week and row on three alternate days.

Take a physical exam once per year.

Take my vitamins and supplements every day.

Drink no more than ten cups of coffee per week.

Drink no more than ten alcoholic drinks per week.

Knowledge Sphere:

I want to continually learn new things and to be an accomplished entrepreneur, an effective educator, and an excellent communicator to and for society. I want to be exposed to new cultural experiences without feeling compelled to tout these experiences unless they are valued by someone.

My Goals

I will study "Conscious Leadership" during 2005.

I will study astronomy during 2005.

By December 31, I will be reasonably fluent in Czech.

My Actions

Read at least two books per month, one on science, one on leadership. I read two hours per day and thirty minutes before retiring to bed (11:00 p.m.).

Peruse/read two newspapers per day and ten journals per month.

Build my collection of rare technical books and antique technical instruments, especially when I travel to other places.

Go away one weekend per month with Inez.

Take Czech lessons two hours per week and study Czech one hour per day.

Travel with Inez to one place on my "Itinerary List" every one to two years.

Itinerary List: (Bold have been visited): **Grand Canyon**, Yellowstone, **Yosemite, Oregon, New England, Africa (Kenya, Tanzania, Mt. Kilimanjaro, South Africa**, Egypt), Israel, **Turkey, Greece**, Nepal, Tibet, **India**, China, **Brazil**, Argentina, Machu Picchu, Australia, and Alaska.

Buy a small telescope by June 30 and use it once per week for at least one hour.

Time Management:

My Goal

Without being fanatical and overbearing, I manage my life in a manner that provides personal and professional balance and helps me to achieve, in the most effective manner, all of the goals I have set for myself.

My Actions

Every weekend, I evaluate my performance against the plan and make adjustments.

I leave my comfort zone at least once per day.

I set deadlines for all vital tasks and say no to tasks that are not vital.

I never say in one hundred words what can be said in ten.

I accept what I cannot change as facts of life.

I spend fifteen minutes every morning planning my day.

Appendix B

Relaxation and Meditation

The strategies described in this book have more effective results if pursued in parallel with the development and practice of your spiritual character through meditation. I therefore thought it helpful to offer a brief description of meditation for those not versed in these procedures. However, it should not be considered as an alternative to a serious study of relaxation and meditation techniques, especially under the guidance of an appropriate teacher.

Relaxation

According to *Raja Yoga*, developed in India a few thousand years ago, the spinal column contains two primary nerve currents—the *Ida* path on the left of the column and the *Pingala* path on the right. There is also a central passageway within the spinal column called "Sushumna." The two nerve current pathways are key to facilitating movement through the Sushumna passageway of the *Kundalini*, which according to Raja Yoga physiology is a huge reserve of consciousness energy, situated at the base of the spine.

In Sanskrit, Kundalini means "coiled up." This energy is difficult to arouse and takes much practice to do so. However, when it is aroused and released, it is said to travel up the spine through six centers or lotuses of consciousness, reaching the seventh center, located at the core of your brain. As the Kundalini energy reaches higher centers, it produces increasing degrees of enlightenment—the seventh level inducing intense bliss, which is experienced usually only by those well practiced in relaxation and meditation techniques.

There are advanced breathing procedures called *Pranayama*, which are designed to arouse and release the Kundalini energy; however, in the hands of uninformed or unpracticed individuals, these procedures can be very dangerous. Used improperly, they can cause physical and mental impairment and worse.

There is, however, a well-known procedure that is most helpful in achieving relaxation quite quickly. It involves only modest arousal of the Kundalini energy and can be easily practiced by anyone as follows:

- ❖ Find a quiet place where you will not be disturbed by anyone or anything. Sit comfortably in the lotus position, or if that is uncomfortable, use a chair with a rigid back support. It is fine to lean back, however the spine must remain erect even though you are in a relaxed position.

- ❖ Close your eyes and depress the right nostril with the thumb of your right hand and breathe in deeply through your left nostril. Try to do this smoothly over a period of about ten seconds. As you inhale focus on the air you are inhaling as containing pure conscious energy (Prana). Envision it as a life-breath sending a current of energy down the Ida nerve bundle to your Kundalini situated in a triangular lotus at the base of your spine.

- ❖ Hold your breath for about ten seconds, mentally repeating your mantra, if you have one. If not, use the universal sacred mantra, OM. Or, if you prefer, you can use the Hindu Sanskrit mantra, *Sat, Chit, Ananda,* which translates, Existence, Consciousness, Bliss. During this period allow the Prana to stimulate the Kundalini.

- ❖ As you release the right nostril, close the left nostril with your forefinger and slowly exhale the air in your lungs through your right nostril, envisioning as you do so that you are expelling negative energy and spiritual or conscious impurities from your body. You might even envision smoke emitting from your nostril making your body, mind, and consciousness achieve a cleaner state of being.

- ❖ Keeping your left nostril closed, now inhale slowly over ten seconds through the right nostril, filling your lungs to capacity and sending a current of Prana energy down the Pingala nerve bundle adjacent to your spine directly to the Kundalini and stimulate as before.

- ❖ Continue this process for ten minutes, alternating nostril closure.

This technique is safe to practice and is known to moderately stimulate the Kundalini energy situated at the base of your spine. It is a powerful tool for relaxation and preparation for meditation.

Meditation

Your can find any number of books which explain the practice, purpose, and physiological effects of meditation. However, a simple yet effective means to meditation is as follows:

- ❖ Practice the above-described relaxation technique for ten minutes.

- ❖ Continue to sit in the same lotus position, or on a chair, maintaining your eyes closed.

- ❖ Bring your mental focus to your heart—not your biological heart, but the center of your chest, just adjacent to your physical heart. Breathe normally.

- ❖ Imagine a bright light source coming from a distance into your heart.

- ❖ It is also helpful, although not necessary, to focus your mind on your mantra while you have this vision. If you have no mantra at this time, use the Indian sacred mantra, OM.

- ❖ In the beginning and even periodically after you have practiced meditation for some time, your focus will be broken by mundane thoughts, very much as we experience all of the time. "What is my schedule today?" "I wonder if Bob will be at work today." "Gee, I would love to try that new Chinese restaurant." This mental chatter is normal, especially when you first begin to practice meditation. The most important thing is NOT to let it bother you. Simply and casually regain your focus on your mantra. In the Eastern Wisdom Traditions, these thoughts are said to result from *Samskaras*, imprints on your mind, which must be released to achieve consistent and constant focus on the NOW.

- ❖ In the beginning, meditate for about twenty minutes. After a few weeks, increase to thirty minutes, and after a few more weeks, increase to forty-five and then to sixty minutes. That is sufficient. However, even twenty minutes per day, preferably in the early morning, is sufficient to have significant benefits.

- ❖ To the extent that it is practical, practice your relaxation and meditation techniques in the same place and at the same time each day.

❖ A variation of these techniques is to practice relaxation in the evening before going to bed, and meditation in the morning after bathing, but before dressing and breakfast. This is best done when all others are either asleep or in a separate part of the house.

Both of these techniques, if practiced faithfully and carefully, can bring excellent results.

Appendix C

Vision, Mission, Values, and Dream of Chateau Mcely

Our Vision
We make a difference in the world by making a difference in the lives of our guests and fellow teammates.

Our Mission
Our mission is to support our guests and teammates towards their highest personal potential through a balance of body, mind, and spirit.

Our Promise
We are dedicated to providing our guests with the highest level of service and comfort.

Our Picture
A cozy, relaxed friendly atmosphere with the service of an international leading hotel.

Our Dream
Create a better world by enriching the lives of our guests and employees.

Chateau Mcely's Team Values

1. **We continuously surprise our guests.**
   We are dedicated to providing outstanding services to our guests. No request is too large for us. When our guests leave Chateau Mcely, we want them to feel like they have been treated with genuine friendliness, kindness, and concern for their needs.

2. **We practice integrity and mutual respect in all that we do.**
   We are always honest with each other and with our clients, and we always show the highest respect for the other person. We know that each of us is a precious and powerful link in a very strong chain.

3. **We seek and appreciate feedback from team members and guests.**

We know that the only way we can grow as a person and as a team is to have honest two-way feedback among our team members. We don't all have the same needs, desires, and skills, but we know when these needs, desires, and skills are respected and seamlessly meshed together, we create a powerful team that can accomplish much for the small number of people on our team.

4. **We seek the Joy of Life for clients, team members, and ourselves.**

We understand that life is precious, and we also know that our challenging world often clouds the Joy-of-Life in people's everyday affairs. We want to change that for our clients when they are at Chateau Mcely. We know that besides great service, we must also personally exude the Joy in our own lives as we work with our teammates to create this environment.

5. **We solve challenging problems together.**

There is nothing more powerful than the synergy of a well-tuned team in solving challenging problems. Under these conditions two plus two is always much greater than four. That is why we draw on the combined creativity and ingenuity of our team members in solving tough problems—no matter how difficult or sensitive the problem may be.

6. **We are a learning organization.**

We know that knowledge is power, and this is the century of the knowledge worker. We continuously seek knowledge and its use with good judgment, i.e., we develop and practice the power of wisdom. The only way that we can compete effectively in this world is to continuously improve ourselves and our team through learning.

7. **We focus on the Triple Bottom Line—People, Planet, Profit.**

We focus on people—our stakeholders—as they are our most important asset and critical to our Dream. We also believe that everything on this beautiful planet is somehow connected, and we seek to use its resources in a way that makes it a better world. We know that when you take care of planet and people, profit always follows.

8. We work as a family.

We understand that no two family members are alike, nor do they have the same needs. We respect these differences, and when it comes to important issues we are "all for one and one for all."

Notes

Foreword

1 Charles A. Cusumano, Sr., the author's deceased father.

Preface

2 Paulo Coelho, *The Alchemist, 10th Anniversary Edition* (New York: HarperOne, 1993). Kindle Edition, Location 321.

Part I | MY STORY

Chapter 1: *On the Shoulders of Giants*

3 Isaac Newton, in a letter to physicist Sir Robert Hooke, February 15, 1676.

4 James A. Cusumano, Cosmic Consciousness: *A Journey to Well-being, Happiness, and Success* (Prague: Fortuna Libri Press, 2011).

5 Lynne McTaggart, *The Intention Experiment: Using Your Thoughts to Change Your Life and The World* (New York: Free Press, 2007).

6 Don't try any of these experiments at home. They are very, very dangerous, and can be, and often have been deadly!

7 The U.S. ERDA was the predecessor to the current U.S. Department of Energy (DOE).

8 The astute observer will notice that XONON is NO NO_x spelled backwards!

9 "What Matters Most," Feature Film, http://www.chateauwallyfilms.biz/ (http://www.imdb.com/title/tt0266041/).

10 Jane Cusumano, http://www.imdb.com/name/nm0193824/.

11 Polly Cole, http://www.imdb.com/name/nm0193826/.

12 Richard W. Munchkin, *Gambling Wizards: Conversations with the World's Greatest Gamblers* (New York: Huntington Press, 2003).

13 *Forbes* Magazine.

14 The Thurn Taxis family invented the concept of the postal system in Europe during the Middle Ages, and this was the primary source of their wealth. They at first operated it using horse and messenger transport, very much like the Pony Express system in early America.

15   Inez Cusumano, *Chateau Mcely: Honey, Silk, and Pearls* (Prague: Chateau Mcely Press, 2007).

16   Inez and James Cusumano, *The Rebirth of Chateau Mcely*, Documentary film, 2006; http://www.ChateauMcely.com.

17   Small Luxury Hotels of the World, www.SLH.com.

18   Einstein's famous quote, often formulated as, "We cannot solve problems at the same level of consciousness at which they were created."

19   http://www.tripadvisor.com/Hotel_Review-g274707-d626771-Reviews-Chateau_Mcely-Prague_Bohemia.html.

20   Mcely Bouquet Cosmetics, www.McelyBouquet.com.

21   Nely is the Czech spelling for the English Nelly or Nellie.

22   www.ChateauMcelyForum.com.

23   Leadership For Life, www.LeadershipForLife.cz.

24   Inspirational Leadership® is a registered trademark to Dr. Lance W. Secretan.

Part II | Creating a Fulfilling Life

Chapter 2: *Finding Your Purpose and Passion*

25   Paulo Coelho, *The Alchemist,* 10th Anniversary Edition (New York: HarperOne, 1993), Kindle Edition, Location 308.

26   Ricardo B. Levy, *Letters to a Young Entrepreneur* (San Francisco: Catalytic Publishers, 2010).

27   Glenda Burgess, *The Geography of Love: A Memoir* (New York: Broadway Books, 2008) p. 6.

28   Gary Hamel, Gary Hamel's Management 2.0, "Management's Dirty Little Secret," *Wall Street Journal*, December 16, 2009.

29   John Cuber and Peggy B. Harrof, http://www.escholarship.org/editions/view?docId=kt9z09q84w&chunk.id=ss2.02&toc.depth=100&toc.id=ss1.35&brand=ucpress.

30   Gay Hendricks, *Making the Big Leap.* (New York: Harper Collins, 2009).

31   A.H. Maslow, "A Theory of Human Motivation," *Psychological Review* 50(4) (1943): 370-96.

32   Viktor Frankl, (I. Lasch, translator) *Man's Search for Meaning: An Introduction to Logotherapy.* (New York: Washington Square Press, 1963. First published in German in 1946).

33   Clayton Christensen, Curtis W. Johnson and Michael B. Horn, *Disruptive Class, Expanded Edition: How Disruptive Innovation Will Change the Way the World Learns,* 2nd Edition (New York: McGraw-Hill, 2010).

34 Op. cit., Gay Hendricks.

35 James A. Cusumano, performance in Bratislava, Slovakia, http://www.youtube. com/watch?v=5P5HMvfblX4.

Chapter 3: *Creating Your Life Plan*

36 Henry David Thoreau, *Walden: Life in the Woods*, originally published in 1854—Kindle Edition, location 4137, Waxkeep Publishing, January 25, 2013.

37 Margaret Silf, *Inner Compass: An Invitation to Ignatian Spirituality*, 10th Anniversary Edition (Chicago: Loyola Press, 2007).

38 Ibid.

39 Op. cit., James A. Cusumano.

Chapter 4: *Lasting Happiness*

40 Eleanor Roosevelt, *You Learn by Living: Eleven Keys for a More Fulfilling Life* (Louisville, KY: Westminster John Knox Press, 1960) p. 95.

41 Jonathan Haidt, *The Happiness Hypothesis: Finding Modern Truth in Ancient Wisdom* (New York: Basic Books, 2006) p. 90ff.

42 M. E. P. Seligman, *Authentic Happiness* (New York: Free Press, 2002).

43 Op. cit., Jonathan Haidt, p. 92.

44 S. Frederick and G. Loewenstein, *Hedonic Adaptation*. In D. Kahneman, E. Diener and N. Schwartz (Eds.) *Well-being. The Foundations of Hedonic Psychology.* (New York: Russell Sage Press, 1999).

45 M. Koslowsky, A. N. Kluger and Mordechai Reich, *Commuting Stress: Causes, Effects and Methods of Coping* (New York: Plenum Press, 1995).

46 Jonathan Haidt and J. Rodin, "Control and Efficacy of Interdisciplinary Bridges," *Review of General Psychology* 3 (1999) 317-37.

47 J. Rodin and E. Langer, *Journal of Personality and Social Psychology* 35 (1977) 897-902.

48 Sonja Lyubomirsky, Laura King, and Ed Diener, "The Benefits of Frequent Positive Affect: Does Happiness Lead to Success?" *Psychological Bulletin* 131 (2005): 803–55.

49 H. T. Reis and S. L. Gable, "Toward a Positive Psychology of Relationships," in C. L. M. Keyes and J. Haidt (Eds.), *Flourishing, Positive Psychology and the Life Well-lived*, American Psychological Association, (Washington D.C.: 2002), 129-59.

50 Denise Mann, "Loneliness, Living Alone Might Shorten Life," http://health. usnews.com/health-news/news/articles/2012/06/18/loneliness-living-alone-might-shorten-life.

51 Jeffrey Sachs, "In Search of Equilibrium," *New York Times*, December 2, 2010.

52 Prabhat Pankaj and Tshering Dorji, "Measuring Individual Happiness in Relation to Gross National Happiness in Bhutan: Some Preliminary Results from Survey Data," Center For Bhutan Studies, September 1, 2011.

53 Op. cit., Gary Hamel.

54 Martin Seligman, www.AuthenticHappiness.org.

55 Lance Secretan, www.Secretan.com.

56 Op. cit., J. Rodin and E. Langer.

57 Op. cit., Jonathan Haidt, p. 238.

58 Stanford University commencement address by Steve Jobs, CEO of Apple Computer and of Pixar Animation Studios, delivered on June 12, 2005.

59 Ibid.

Chapter 5: *The Power of Passion, the Fallacy of Fear*

60 John C. Maxwell, *The Maxwell Daily Reader* (Nashville, TN: Thomas Nelson Publishers, 2007), Kindle Edition, Location 556.

61 Oil Change International, http://priceofoil.org/.

62 E. O. Wilson, "The Bottleneck," *Scientific American*, February 2002.

63 This wording adapted from a book on Inspirational Leadership by Lance Secretan, *The Spark, the Flame and the Torch: Change yourself. Change the World.* (Secretan Center Press, 2010).

64 Op. cit., Gary Hamel.

65 Opt. cit., Gary Hamel.

66 http://www.cbc.ca/news/indepth/words/misquotes.html, Most sources quote Armstrong as saying, "That's one small step for man; one giant step for mankind," which is grammatically incorrect. He actually said "a man" but the transmission was distorted and the "a" was not reproduced clearly.

67 Op. cit., James A. Cusumano.

Part III | Building a Successful Business

Chapter 6: *Building a Successful Company*

68   Vince Lombardi, with permission of the Luminary Group LLC, http://www.vincelombardi.com/licensing2.html.

69   We also formed a third business unit, Catalytica Advanced Technologies (CAT), which addressed rapid throughput and screening of new catalytic systems for the efficient development of new catalytic processes. It eventually morphed into a company called NovoDynamics. However, our primary focus was in CPI and CESI.

70 Op. cit., Reference 63 for an excellent description of Inspired Leadership.

71 Op. cit., Reference 63, p. 88.

72 Op. cit., Ricardo B. Levy, Kindle Edition, Location 241-243.

73 http://school-for-champions.com/speeches/churchill_never_give_in.htm: On October 29, 1941, United Kingdom (Great Britain) Prime Minister Winston Churchill visited Harrow School to hear the traditional songs he had sung there as a youth, as well as to speak to the students. This became one of his most quoted speeches, due to distortions that evolved about what he actually said. The myth is that Churchill stood before the students and said, "Never, ever, ever, ever, ever, ever, ever, give in. Never give in. Never give in. Never give in." Then he sat down. In reality, he made a complete speech that included words similar to what are often quoted. Also, some have stated that he said, "Never give up," which is not correct.

Here is the relevant part of Churchill's actual speech: "But for everyone, surely, what we have gone through in this period—I am addressing myself to the School—surely from this period of ten months, this is the lesson: Never give in. Never give in. Never, never, never, never—in nothing, great or small, large or petty—never give in, except to convictions of honor and good sense. Never yield to force. Never yield to the apparently overwhelming might of the enemy."

74 "Measuring Social Impact: The Foundation of Social Return on Investment (SROI)," London School of Business, http://sroi.london.edu/Measuring-Social-Impact.pdf.

Chapter 7: *Inspirational Leadership*®

75 Lance Secretan, *The Spark, the Flame, and the Torch: Inspire Self. Inspire Others. Inspire the World* (Caledon, Ontario, Canada: The Secretan Center Inc., 2010), Kindle Edition—Location 85.

76 The term Inspirational Leadership®, a register trademark by Lance Secretan, is sometimes used in the literature interchangeably with the term Conscious Leadership.

77 CASTLE Principles™ is a trademark applied for by Lance Secretan and the Secretan Center Inc.

78 Much of the substantive content of this chapter is based on the CASTLE Principles™, which have been developed by Dr. Lance H. K. Secretan. See for example, "ONE—The Art and Practice of Conscious Leadership," (The Secretan Center, 2006). I have found these principles closest to my own way of thinking and operating over the years and a powerful tool in creating a successful, fulfilling, and gratifying organization.

79 Op. cit., Reference 63.

80 James C. Humes, *The Wit & Wisdom of Winston Churchill* (New York: HarperCollins, 1995), Kindle Edition, Location 429.

81 Op. cit., Reference 63.

82 Ibid.

83 Ibid, p. 112.

84 James A. Autry, *The Servant Leader: How to Build a Creative Team, Develop Great Morale, and Improve Bottom-Line Performance* (New York: Three Rivers Press, 2001), Kindle Edition, Location 327.

85 Chicago Tylenol Murders, http://en.wikipedia.org/wiki/Chicago Tylenol murders, page was last modified on October 11, 2012.

86 Ibid.

87 Henry Ford, *My Life and Work*, (North Charleston, South Carolina: CreateSpace Independent Publishing Platform, 2011).

88 "First Force" here refers to something responsible for the Big Bang which occurred about 13.7 billion years ago and gave birth to everything in the universe—all matter and all energy. It is likely not a force as we know it in the sense of classical physics.

89 Op. cit., James A. Cusumano.

90 Ibid.

91 These values are presented in expanded form in the Appendix C.

92 Helen Schucman, *A Course in Miracles*, Third Edition, (Mill Valley, CA: Foundation for Inner Peace Publishers, 2007) T-31. VI.

93 Op. cit., Reference 78, p. 125.

94 George Sand, pseudonym for novelist Amantine Lucile Dupin, Encyclopedia Britannica, personal letter, 1862.

95 Op. cit. Reference 63, p. 159.

96 Op. cit., Reference 63, p. 160.

97 Peter F. Drucker, *Management: Tasks, Responsibilities, Practices* (New York: Harper Business, 1993) 44.

98 Op. cit., Reference 63, 163-4.

99 Op. cit., James A. Cusumano.

Chapter 8: *Power Performance Reviews*

100 Gary Hamel with Bill Breen, "An Agenda for Management Innovation," *Harvard Business Review Shortcuts*, excerpted from *The Future of Management by Gary Hamel with Bill Breen*, Chapter 3 (Boston, Massachusetts: Harvard Business School Press, 2007), Kindle Edition, Location 470.

101 For example, see Analytix Strategy and Performance Management http://www.analytix.co.za/Training/Courses/StrategyPerformanceManagement.aspx.

102 Jeffrey Hollender and Bill Breen, *The Responsibility Revolution: How the Next Generation of Business Will Win* (San Francisco: Jossey-Bass, 2010).

103 See: http://www.flickr.com/photos/lindenlab/.

104 Towers Perrin Global Workforce Study, 2007–2008: "Closing the Engagement Gap: A Roadmap for Driving Superior Business Performance," http://www.towersperrin.Com/tp/getwebcachedoc?webc=HRS/USA/2008/200803/GWS_Global_Report20072008_31208.pdf.

105 Gary Hamel, Reference 28.

Chapter 9: *Creating an Innovative Environment*

106 Gary Hamel with Bill Breen, "An Agenda for Management Innovation, *Harvard Business Review Short Cuts*, excerpted from *The Future of Management* by Gary Hamel with Bill Breen, Chapter 3 (Boston: Massachusetts, Harvard Business School Press, 2007), Kindle Edition, Location 258 and 262.

107 Norman McCrae, "Intrapreneurial Now," *Economist*, April 17, 1982.

Chapter 10: *Conscious Capitalism*

108 Vaclav Havel, First President of Czech Republic, *Speech on the Occasion of the Liberty Medal Ceremony, Philadelphia, PA, July 4, 1994.*

109 The World Business Academy, established in 1986, is a great resource for the role of business in addressing the whole (www.WorldBusiness.org).

110 Jared Diamond, *Collapse: How Societies Choose to Fail or Succeed* (Penguin: 2011).

111 Sir Martin Rees, *Our Final Hour: A Scientist's Warning* (London: Basic Books, 2004).

112 Fred Kofman, *Conscious Business: How to Build Value Through Values* (Louisville, Colorado: Sound True, Inc.: 2006), see also http://www.ConsciousCapitalism.com/ and references therein.

113 Rajendra S. Sisodia, David B. Wolfe, and Jagdish N. Sheth, *Firms of Endearment* (Philadelphia: Wharton School Publishing, 2007).

114 Op. cit., Reference 112.

115 See for example, http://www.davidfoster.tv/why-carrot-and-stick-leadership-is-dead/.

116 Op. cit., James A. Cusumano.

117 Op. cit, Reference 63.

118 Op. cit., Reference 28.

119 Op. cit., Reference 78.

120 Op. cit., Reference 63.

121 Charles Johnson, *The Yoga Sutras of Patanjali: The Book of the Spiritual Man,* An Interpretation by Charles Johnson, (New York: Copyright by Charles Johnson, 1912). See also Patanjali, *How to Know God: The Yoga Aphorisms Of Patanjali,* translated with a commentary by Swami Prabhavanda and Christopher Isherwood, (Hollywood, California: Vedanta Press, 1981).

122 OneDream™ is a registered trademark by Lance Secretan and the Secretan Center.

123 Lance Secretan, *The Spark, the Flame and the Torch: Inspire Others. Inspire the World* (The Secretan Center Inc., 2010; released in English June 2010 and in the Czech language in May, 2011).

124 His precise quote was, "If I am not myself, who will be for me? And if I am for myself alone, what am I? And if not now, when?" see http://en.wikipedia.org/wiki/Hillel_the_Elder.

Appendix A: *My Life Plan*

125 I chose to use an older example of my life plan to demonstrate how effective the process can be. Literally, more than 98 percent of the goals set in this 2005 plan were achieved, most of them on time To be frank, the one goal I faltered on, and yet the one for which I have most control, is to maintain my desired weight through diet and exercise. My sweet tooth and zest for wine often get the best of me!

126 *"First Force"* is my way of stating my belief that infinite *"Intelligence"* exists that *is,* always *was,* and always *will be,* and that Intelligence is behind the creation of our universe and all other universes that may exist. It is further my belief that this Intelligent Consciousness is intimately connected with humanity's consciousness, and for that matter with all things material and non-material and works with and through all forces, including mankind, in the continuous physical and conscious evolution of everything in the universe(s). Some would call this God. I don't see this as the God prescribed by organized religions. Because of the intimate connection between Intelligent Consciousness and our own consciousness, I believe that we co-create with Intelligent Consciousness everything that happens in our lives. My thoughts on this are described in detail in my last book, *Cosmic Consciousness: A Journey to Well-being, Happiness and Success* (Prague: Fortuna Libra Press, 2011).

127 Op. cit. Reference 9.

128 See: www.ChateauMcely.com.

129 Op. cit, Reference 22.

130 Op. cit., Reference 23.

Index

Y

Z

About the Author

James A. Cusumano is an accomplished leader with successful careers as an entertainer, scientist, corporate executive, and entrepreneur. He started his professional journey as a successful entertainer as the lead singer for *The Royal Teens* of the 1950s and 1960s "Short-Shorts" and "Short Shorts Twist" fame. After receiving a PhD in physical chemistry, pursuing business studies at Harvard and Stanford, and receiving a fellowship at Churchill College at Cambridge University, he served as a research scientist and then Director of R&D for Exxon. Dr. Cusumano subsequently cofounded Catalytica, Inc., one of Silicon Valley's successful companies with business units in clean energy and pharmaceuticals. He served as President and CEO of Catalytica and then as its Chairman. He also served as Chairman and CEO of Catalytica Pharmaceuticals, Inc., which grew in less than five years from several people to almost 2,000 employees with nearly $500 million in revenue, increasing Catalytica's market value to $1 billion.

Following this, Dr. Cusumano founded Chateau Wally Films and produced *What Matters Most*, released in over fifty countries.[127]

He moved to Prague where he and his wife, Inez, renovated Chateau Mcely into an internationally recognized spa hotel and forest retreat, chosen by the World Travel Awards as The World's Leading Green Hotel.[128]

Dr. Cusumano created Chateau Mcely Forum[129] to provide resources and educational products for Inspired Leadership and Conscious Business. Leadership for Life, a program that brings internationally recognized and accomplished leaders to Prague and Chateau Mcely to teach the power and potential of Inspired Leadership, is but one example of his pursuits in this area.[130] An inspiring speaker and talented entertainer, he is the author of numerous technical and business publications as well as the author of *Cosmic Consciousness: A Journey to Well-being, Happiness and Success*, and a coauthor of *Freedom from Mid-East Oil*.